THE MARLBOROUGH TAPESTRIES
AT BLENHEIM PALACE

Frontispiece: *John Churchill, Duke of Marlborough.*
Detail from the *Battle of Blenheim* (Fig. 42).

The Marlborough Tapestries at Blenheim Palace

AND THEIR RELATION TO OTHER MILITARY TAPESTRIES
OF THE WAR OF THE SPANISH SUCCESSION

by Alan Wace

PHAIDON · LONDON · NEW YORK

ALL RIGHTS RESERVED BY PHAIDON PRESS LTD · 5 CROMWELL PLACE · LONDON SW7
1968

PHAIDON PUBLISHERS INC · NEW YORK
DISTRIBUTORS IN THE UNITED STATES: FREDERICK A. PRAEGER · INC
I I I FOURTH AVENUE · NEW YORK · N.Y. I0003
LIBRARY OF CONGRESS CATALOG CARD NUMBER: 68–I8903

The design on the binding of this book is based on
the coat of arms of the first Duke of Marlborough
surmounting one of the Grinling Gibbons doorways
of carved white marble in the saloon
at Blenheim Palace.

SBN 7I48 I322 2

MADE IN GREAT BRITAIN
PRINTED BY R. & R. CLARK LTD · EDINBURGH
FRONTISPIECE PRINTED BY JOHN SWAIN & SON LTD · BARNET · HERTFORDSHIRE

CONTENTS

FOREWORD

by Arnold Toynbee

THIS is a monograph on a subject that is of lively interest for the cultivated non-specialist public. The subject, besides being fascinating, has, at the same time, a technical side that needs to be expounded by an expert if the layman, however knowledgeable, is to get his full enjoyment out of it by being helped to understand and appreciate it. Alan Wace has done this service for us in this instance, as in others.

He has been able to do it because he was a born archaeologist. The range of his archaeological interests was unusually wide. It extended from the prehistoric pottery of the mainland of Greece through all the successive strata of Mycenae to the modern embroideries of the Greek islands, and hence to embroideries of other schools. His inborn gift for archaeology enabled him to become an adept in everything that he added to his repertory. He was continually adding to this, since, till the end of his life, his curiosity and his intellectual zest did not flag.

I am not competent to add anything to the appreciation of this present piece of his work that has been given by fellow experts of his, but I do know, at first hand, how high his intellectual quality was — and also what a lovable man he was — since, in 1911–12, I was a junior student at the British Archaeological School in Athens when he was the senior student there, and I had the good fortune to enjoy, from then on, the friendship that I made with him then. No wonder that I found a friend in him; for one of the many things that drew one to him was the generous human way in which he aided people, interested in one or other of his own fields, who were younger and less experienced and less eminent than he was.

London, September 1967

7

INTRODUCTORY NOTE

THIS special study of an interrelated group of Flemish military tapestries was made in the nineteen thirties by my husband, Alan Wace, when he was head of the Department of Textiles in the Victoria and Albert Museum. The initial impulse came from queries raised by owners of various panels and in turn was stimulated by Sir Winston Churchill's use, with the aid of the Museum staff, of selected panels from the 'Victories' in Blenheim Palace for illustration in his biography of his famous ancestor, John Churchill, First Duke of Marlborough. Both Sir Winston and Sir George Trevelyan were interested in the progress of the research and they both willingly gave their help.

Publication of the monograph was postponed by the war and by the author's more pressing archaeological commitments, which absorbed his attention until his death in 1957. In editing the manuscript we have preserved as far as possible the original text, in general limiting alterations to known changes of position and ownership of quoted examples.

To the untiring industry and unflagging interest of H. C. Marillier (now also deceased) is largely due the wide range of illustrative examples in this field. Though the actual authorship is not his, his contribution to the research is considerable. His own position as Managing Director of the Morris Tapestry works gave him ample opportunity to become acquainted with private collections. His own album, a scrap-book of pertinent cuttings and photographs, is a valuable asset in the Department of Textiles in the Victoria and Albert Museum.

My special thanks are due to His Grace the Duke of Marlborough for renewing the permission originally granted to my husband to pursue this research and for allowing me to quote from the Blenheim archives.

For sympathetic help and detailed assistance I am indebted to many scholars of various countries. Without the co-operative and hospitable support of Mr. George Wingfield Digby of the Department of Textiles in the Victoria and Albert Museum and his associates, this project (begun originally during my husband's tenure there) could not have been accomplished.

Much detailed information is due to the help of continental museums and scholars: Dr. Gudmund Boesen (Copenhagen), Professor J. Duverger (Ghent), Dr. E. S. Engelstad (Oslo), Herr Jessen (Berlin), Dr. Wend Graf Kalnein (Dresden), Baron C. F. Palmstierna (Sweden), Mr. Milton Samuels of French and Company, New York, Dr. Arno Schönberger and Dr. Sperlich (Berlin), Miss Wencke Slomann (Oslo), Dr. Hans Thoma and Dr. Michael Petzet (Munich and Schleissheim), and Dr. Eva Zimmermann (Karlsruhe).

In the United States my husband and I have had the helpful assistance of Miss Edith Standen of the Metropolitan Museum of Art in New York and Miss Gertrude Townsend of the Boston Museum of Fine Arts. In England I have derived great profit from the advice, on various points of editorial policy, of Miss Veronica Wedgwood, Miss Margaret Toynbee, Professor Arnold Toynbee, and Mr. David Green.

In conclusion it is my pleasant task to acknowledge the patient help and constructive encouragement I have received from the Phaidon Press, in facing the many problems which inevitably arise in editing a scholarly posthumous book.

Athens, October 1967   HELEN WACE

CHAPTER I
EARLY MILITARY TAPESTRIES

THE use of tapestry to commemorate military exploits appears to be of ancient origin. The subjects, from their pageantry, their uniforms or armour, from the contrasts to be found between solemn triumphal processions and men and horses engaged in violent combat, lend themselves almost naturally to such pictorial treatment. As far back as the days of Homer we read of a battle scene between the Greeks and Trojans being woven by Helen, in what was certainly a form of art; and centuries later, in the great era of tapestry under patrons like the Dukes of Burgundy down to the death of Charles the Bold in 1477, military subjects were among the most popular of those chosen for representation. It is true that in that age of religious fervour they were not so much in vogue as sacred scenes or allegories, and that hunting and pastoral themes, with all the simple occupations of daily life, played an equally large part in a society to which books were practically unknown. Moreover, the military scenes chosen for illustration were less those of contemporary achievement than the deeds of famous heroes, mythical or historical.

The best known instance is the great *History of Troy*,[1] a series of incidents based on the romance of Benoît de Saint-More, taken not from Homer, but from Dictys, and reproduced more than once. The finest set was one woven by Pasquier Grenier of Tournai,[2] and presented by the city of Bruges to Charles the Bold. The Louvre possesses the original sketches for the cartoons,[3] and though no complete set survives there are portions of various versions still extant.

In the same category comes the *History of Caesar*[4] at Berne, which dates from about 1450, and formed part of the spoils of Charles the Bold's camp after his disastrous defeat at Grandson by the Swiss.

Slightly later are the *Destruction of Jerusalem by Titus*,[5] extant in a few fragmentary versions, and really forming part of a series of morality tapestries; and the *History of Charlemagne*, with which may be grouped the brilliant Roncesvalles panel[6] in Brussels, woven at Tournai about 1455. In this latter subject, the legends wreathed round the mythical fame of Roland have been freely used to make the history romantic in accordance with the spirit of the age.

A similar idea pervades the interesting tapestries now in the Petit Palais in Paris, illustrating the legend of *Alexander and King Nicholas of Caesarea*,[7] while another aspect of the medieval Alexander romance is represented by the two magnificent panels in the Palazzo Doria in Rome.[8] Yet here, if the suggestion (not in itself improbable) is correct, there has been an attempt to celebrate living men under the guise of heroes of antiquity. In these two subjects, the youthful Alexander and his father Philip bear considerable likeness to the portraits of the youthful Charles the Bold and his father Philip the Good.

Another splendid set which combines historical and mythical elements and is partly military in character is the famous *History of Clovis*, of which only two panels now survive in Rheims Cathedral.[9] This series came into the possession of Charles V as part of the inheritance of the Dukes of Burgundy and was found among the spoils of his abandoned camp when he was forced to raise the siege of Metz in 1552. It became the property of Francis of Guise; and later Charles of Guise, Cardinal of Lorraine, gave it to Rheims Cathedral.

In all these tapestries, just as in the famous *Justice of Trajan*[10] at Berne, the romantic element outweighs the historical and, in accordance with the tendency of the later years of chivalry, legend is preferred to fact and picturesqueness to accuracy, especially when a moral lesson could be introduced at the same time, as in the Trajan and Jerusalem themes.

Still it does not follow that contemporary events were never represented in tapestries of the Middle Ages. One of the first that comes to mind is the set commemorating Du Guesclin, the hero of the French struggle for freedom in the fourteenth century, for his exploits against the English invaders had all the necessary flavour of romance.[11] Another, of the same period, is the great *Battle of Roosebeke*,[12] supplied to Philip 'Le Hardi' by Michael Bernard of Arras in 1386. This survived well into the sixteenth century (when it had been cut into three pieces), but has since disappeared. The battle was fought in 1382 by the Flemings in revolt, headed by Philip van Artevelde, against the Duke of Burgundy, who was assisted by the youthful Charles VI, King of France, and it resulted in an overwhelming victory for the royal forces.

A further notable example of contemporary historical representation is the series depicting the *Conquest of Arzila* by Alphonso V of Portugal ('Africano'), which is now in the Church at Pastrana, near Madrid.[13] There are three panels showing various incidents of the campaign. The panels are crowded with figures of knights in armour, some possibly intended as portraits, and with lances, banners, ships, and all the panoply of medieval warfare. They were taken from Portugal by Philip II of Spain and are popularly supposed to have been given by him to his mistress, who became, or was, a Duchess of Pastrana. They bear a strong resemblance to the Troy tapestries and were doubtless woven at Tournai at about the same date, 1470.

CHAPTER II

THE RENAISSANCE

FROM the sixteenth century onwards there is no lack of true material for a history of military tapestries, and the change of style in weaving from the Gothic, or archaic, to the pictorial manner of the Renaissance afforded greater scope to the artists in their treatment of contemporary events. The change, of course, was gradual, and represents an evolution or transition rather than a sudden break. Thus the Spitzer panel at the Gobelins Museum of *Louis XI raising the Siege of Dôle* (or Salins),[1] which formed one of a large series in the church of St. Anatoile at Salins and was woven at Bruges between 1501 and 1506, is frankly and unmistakably Gothic, both in conception and in execution. *The Siege of Dijon*[2] in the museum of that town, commemorating Dijon's escape from the Swiss attack in 1513, is transitional, while the full development of the Renaissance style is shown in the two great sets of tapestries woven for the Emperor Charles V —one depicting the campaign which ended in the capture of Francis I at the *Battle of Pavia* in 1525 (Fig. 1), and the other illustrating the *Conquest of Tunis* (Fig. 2).

The *Battle of Pavia* set[3] was presented to the Emperor by the Netherlands to commemorate his victory. Don Carlos, son of Philip II, and grandson of Charles V, bequeathed it to his tutor, Don Horatio Juan, and the last of the Avalos family gave

1. *The Battle of Pavia*, woven for the Emperor Charles V. Naples, National Museum.

or bequeathed it to the Naples Museum in 1862. It consists now of seven subjects, the cartoons for which were designed by the Flemish master Bernard van Orley, better known as the artist of the *Hunts of Maximilian*.[4] The sketches for the *Battle of Pavia*[5] series are in the Louvre, and show the combatants dressed in the trunk hose costume of the period, as they appear in the tapestries (Fig. 1).

Round the *Conquest of Tunis* tapestries a literature has grown up,[6] owing both to the unique wealth of detailed information we possess about the contract with the Brussels weavers and to the fact that the original cartoons still exist and form one of the treasures of the State Collections in Vienna. The Emperor Charles V himself supplied all the wool, silk, and gold and silver thread required for their execution and imposed the most rigid conditions for their manufacture. The cartoons, twelve in number, were designed by the court painter Jan Vermeyen, who accompanied the expedition, and the weaver was the famous Wilhelm Pannemaker, on whose looms were woven so many of the finest tapestries now extant. The tapestries were brought to England to enhance the decorations at the wedding of the Emperor's son Philip and Mary Tudor, and were in such general demand for similar functions that they fell into decay. They were consequently replaced by a set of smaller dimensions also woven by Pannemaker. This set, of which ten survive, was in its turn supplemented in the eighteenth century by a copy woven at Madrid by Van der Goten in 1740 to the order of Philip V. By the time this set was required, the original cartoons were no longer available, and the replica had to be woven from the ten surviving panels of the smaller Pannemaker series. These two sets form an important part of the tapestry collection of the Crown of Spain.

The later history of the cartoons is curious and may be found in an anecdote related by Marshal Count Mérode-Westerloo.[7] When he was with the Emperor Charles VI at Innsbruck, in November 1711, their conversation turned to the designs for the *Conquest of Tunis*, which the Emperor said he remembered having been shown as a boy by his father Leopold on their discovery at Vienna and which had been erroneously attributed to Titian.[8] He suggested that the best of the Flemish weavers should be consulted as to their reproduction, and ordered the cartoons themselves to be looked out and dispatched to Frankfurt.[9] The Marshal for his part sent for the Brussels weaver, Judocus de Vos,[10] with the result that a completely modernized set of the tapestries was produced for the Austrian State Collection. The order for this set is on record dated March 10th, 1712, but the tapestries were not delivered until 1721.

Another great series of military tapestries belonging to the Crown of Spain represents the *Victories of the Archduke Albert* won in 1596 in a campaign against Henry IV of France.[11] It consists of seven pieces woven by Martin Reymbouts of Brussels from cartoons by Jan Snellinck (1544–1638), court painter to the Archduke (1559–1621), and in accordance with old custom was a gift from the city of Antwerp in honour of their

2. *The Sortie from Goletta* (detail), from the *Conquest of Tunis* series, woven for the Emperor Charles V. Madrid, Royal Palace.

new ruler. The Spanish troops are depicted in the typical costume of the period with puffed and pointed jerkins and trunk hose or breeches.

The *Victories of the Duke of Alva*, conqueror of the Netherlands, are similarly represented in a series of tapestries woven by Wilhelm Pannemaker, of which three were in the possession of his descendant, the present Duke of Alva.[12]

At the Musée du Cinquantenaire in Brussels there is an interesting frieze of the *Battle of Nieuport*, fought in 1600 by Prince Maurice of Nassau against the Archduke Albert. It is a seventeenth-century piece, ordered from Maximilian van der Gucht of Delft in 1647, and is surrounded by a highly decorative border containing the arms of the seventeen provinces and views of Flemish and Dutch cities in medallions.[13] It is a striking piece and of great historical as well as artistic value.

Battle subjects were among the huge series of twenty-seven tapestries woven in memory of Henry III of France at the Château de Cadillac, near Bordeaux, by his favourite, the Duc d'Epernon.[14] The name of the chief weaver, Claude de la Pierre,

15

who wove the tapestries between 1632 and 1637, has been preserved, but of the set itself all has perished or disappeared except a fragment or two and one known panel, now in the Louvre, representing the *Battle of Jarnac*, fought in 1569. The latter is a vigorous, but rather crude example of a battle scene with bodies of heavily armed cavalry charging each other, solid blocks of infantry, and individual protagonists marked with their names, such as Condé, De Châtilhon, and De la Valette, in situations showing the part they bore in the engagement. The set, which as the dates show was woven many years after the events depicted, was bought by Louis XIV at the sale of the effects of a Duc d'Epernon in 1682, and figured in crown inventories until the French Revolution, when it was lost to sight.[15]

There are three coarser provincial tapestries of the same subjects, *Battle of Jarnac* (two phases) and *Battle of St. Denis*, in the Cluny Museum. Compared with the d'Epernon piece they are childish in drawing and composition, all the figures being of one size and recalling the manœuvres of lead soldiers, especially the solid blocks of pikemen. The principal figures and details of the battle are named and labelled much in the style of the Italian *vedute prospettive*.

Various towns of Holland have preserved the memory of military or naval engagements in which their citizens distinguished themselves by means of tapestries exhibited in the town halls. At Middelburg,[16] for example, in the Council Chamber, there are six pieces of which five depict the sixteenth-century naval battles between the Spaniards and the Dutch (Fig. 3). Except for one woven by Franz Spierincx at Delft, they were the work from 1595 onwards of the family of De Maecht, of whom one member, Philip, is notable for having helped to found the pre-Gobelins industry in Paris, under Henry IV. He was afterwards induced to come to England in order to start the Mortlake tapestry works in 1619.

Haarlem possesses in its town hall a single piece showing the *Capture of Damietta*, which was woven by one J. Thibout about 1630.[17] As the tapestry illustrates an exploit of William of Holland in the Fourth Crusade in 1219, it is a reminder of past glory rather than a record of recent or contemporary success. It shows the Christian vessels, led by a Haarlem cog under full sail, breaking into the Saracen harbour under a hail of arrows and other missiles from the defenders in the towers guarding the entrance between the moles.

Leyden has a piece woven by Joost van Lanckaert of Delft in the late sixteenth century to commemorate its heroic siege and relief in 1574.[18] The tapestry, now in the Leyden Museum, was ordered following a resolution of the city council on February 24th, 1587; it is a curious map-like representation of the event and gives the impression of having been designed from an aeroplane.

The Spierincx of Delft who wove the *Battle of Bergen* (the first of the Middelburg

3. *Sixteenth-century naval battle between the Spaniards and the Dutch.* Middelburg, Council Chamber.

series) after the designs of Hendrick Vroom was also commissioned by Lord Howard of Effingham on behalf of Queen Elizabeth to weave the historic *Armada* tapestries.[19] This famous set of ten panels, which adorned the House of Lords from the time of Cromwell until it perished in the disastrous fire of 1834, was also designed by Hendrick Vroom. It may seem typical of British methods that these national tapestries should have been ordered from abroad when the Sheldon looms at Barcheston and Bordesley were capable of their production, for the famous tapestry maps belonging to the Bodleian Library date apparently from 1588.[20] It is probable, however, that the English looms had not yet acquired sufficient reputation to be entrusted with an undertaking of such importance.

Another famous naval victory of the sixteenth century which was commemorated by a set of tapestries was the *Battle of Lepanto*, won by the fleet of the Holy League under Don John of Austria against the Turks in 1571. In the Palazzo Doria in Rome there is a fine set of Brussels workmanship, perhaps the only one ever woven, consisting of eight panels illustrating this decisive victory. It is said that the tapestries were presented to

17

Admiral Gianandrea Doria by Philip II for the services he rendered in the battle in command of the Genoese squadron.

In Bavaria the Elector Palatine Otto Heinrich (1556–9) had three tapestries woven within his dominion, perhaps at Neuburg, about 1543. These panels, which cannot now be traced, commemorated the part which his brother Philip took in defending Vienna against the Turks in 1529 and in the siege of Langen.[21] Later, between 1605 and 1615, Hans van der Biest wove at Munich to the order of Maximilian I ten large panels from cartoons by Peter de Witte[22] depicting the *History of Otto of Wittelsbach*. Four show battle scenes, the *Storming of a Castle at Verona*, the *Siege of Milan*, the *Descent on Ferrara*, and the *Battle against Henry the Lion*. They deal, however, with events of the twelfth century, and instead of being records of contemporary or recent events, are designed to perpetuate the memory of ancestors, like the fine collection of battle tapestries belonging to the princely house of Thurn and Taxis in Regensburg. They are fanciful reconstructions of family history representing the conflicts of the Visconti and Torriani for the lordship of Milan in the thirteenth and fourteenth centuries and were woven at Brussels in the late seventeenth century by P. van der Borcht and G. van Leefdael. The subjects are elaborate and vigorously conceived, displaying an evident influence of the *Scipio* series after Giulio Romano, and in one case a reminiscence of the Ponte Molle incident from the Rubens *History of Constantine*. Under the influence of these two great artists, the late sixteenth century and the seventeenth produced an overwhelming quantity of classical subjects in tapestry, based largely on Plutarch and Livy, in which battle scenes figure prominently. They are distinguished by a somewhat ferocious realism.

CHAPTER III

THE REIGN OF LOUIS XIV

THE great age of military tapestries, which eclipses all that had gone before, opens with the reign of Louis XIV (1643–1715), who made free use of this art to immortalize the splendour of his achievements and employed for this purpose the newly established royal factories at the Gobelins and at Beauvais. In the forefront must be reckoned the magnificent *Histoire du Roi*[1] composed by C. le Brun and Adam van der Meulen, which among its fourteen panels included seven military episodes, the *Capture of Dôle*, the *Reduction of Dunkirk*, the *Siege of Douai*, the *Taking of Lille*, the *Defeat of the Spaniards at Bruges*, the *Capture of Tournai*, and the *Reduction of Marsal*. The set was begun at the Gobelins by Jans and other weavers in 1665 and the subjects were designed to show the monarch in his glory, usually on a prancing steed, surrounded by a glittering staff and occupying the place of honour in the foreground, while the actions which give their name to the tapestries are relegated to a small scale in the distance. This form of composition, as we shall see, was destined to inaugurate a very popular fashion.

Nor was Louis content with this one tribute to his military prowess. Another set of tapestries, richly woven with gold and silver like the last, was designed by Van der Meulen with the assistance of his pupil Jean Baptiste Martin ('Martin des Batailles') to illustrate his conquests, *Les Conquêtes de Louis le Grand*, and was produced under Béhagle at Beauvais.[2] The original set was made for the Hôtel de Toulouse in Paris, and to this may have belonged five panels recorded in the inventory of Louis-Philippe and sold in 1852, the *Capture of Duisburg*, the *Capture of Besançon*, the *Sortie from Ghent*, the *Sortie from Dôle*, and the *Relief of Messina*, a solitary naval piece. Two of these seem to be those which later came into the possession of Signor Candido Cassini of Florence. A *Battle of Cassel* is at Versailles and a *Capture of Marsal* was sold in Paris in 1903. The largest set, however, seems to have been that bearing the arms of Count von Brühl. Seven panels from it were owned by Lord Amherst of Hackney and later came into the possession of French and Company of New York. They include the *Capture of Duisburg* (Fig. 4) and the *Sortie from Dôle*.[3] Another of the Von Brühl set, said to represent Turenne at the head of his cavalry, is in the Garde-Meuble in Paris, and a ninth panel from it, the *Relief of Messina*, appeared at a sale in Paris in 1912.

These two series are both designed in the grand style of the great artists who composed them, and being woven in wool, silk, and gold thread by the best craftsmen of the age, are decorative pieces of the first order, well adapted for their aim, which was to portray the greatness and the magnificence of Le Roi Soleil.

4. *The Capture of Duisburg*, woven for Louis XIV. New York, French and Company.

One of the earliest rulers to emulate Louis XIV in the glorification of his military achievements by means of tapestry was the Great Elector, Frederick William of Brandenburg (1640–88). In 1686 an Aubusson weaver named Pierre Mercier had settled in Berlin, and to him was entrusted the mission of illustrating the Elector's *Victories over the Swedes* (1675–9).[4] The cartoons were designed by the painters Langefeld and Casteels. Before the Second World War the set of six tapestries hung in the palace in Berlin, then used to house the collections of the Kunstgewerbemuseum. The tapestries now belong

20

to the Department of State Palaces and Gardens, and are housed in the Palace of Charlottenburg in West Berlin. They contain a profusion of silver thread, much tarnished. The style of the designs reflects the influence of Le Brun, although the military operations are on a larger scale. The borders are florid, interspersed with groups of trophies, and have armorial bearings on three sides. In the centre of the lower border is a Latin title in a cartouche, and one panel bears the weaver's date, 1693. The subjects, in chronological order, are the *Capture of Wolgast* and *Battle of Fehrbellin*, 1675 (Fig. 5); the *Fall of Stettin*, 1677; the *Reduction of Stralsund* and *Landing at Rügen*, 1678; the *Prussian Winter Campaign* (on the ice), 1679.

5. *The Battle of Fehrbellin*, woven for the Great Elector, Frederick William of Brandenburg. Berlin, Palace of Charlottenburg.

Even before the reign of Louis XIV, another northern monarch, Christian IV of Denmark (1588–1648), ordered a great set of tapestries to celebrate his triumph over Sweden in the War of Kalmar (1611–13). These were woven by Karel van Mander of Delft, between 1617 and 1620, and comprised no less than twenty-six panels. They adorned the Great Hall of the Castle of Frederiksborg and perished in the great fire there in 1859.[5] This series was almost entirely military and included among the subjects the *Capture of Kalmar*, the *Defeat of the Swedes at Risbye*, the *Seafight of September 1st, 1611*, the *Landing in Westgothland*, the *Siege of Elfburg*, the *Occupation of Øland*, the *Capture of Borkholm*, the *Capture of Guldburg*, and the *Battle of Travemunde*. The individual panels, no less important artistically than historically, seem to have provided a vivid picture of the costumes and customs of contemporary soldiery. They were well designed and brilliantly executed by one of the best tapestry weavers of the age, and their destruction is a most serious loss.

The Swedes felt that their defeat in this war by their hereditary enemies the Danes was a humiliation, and considered that the existence of this set of tapestries hurt their national pride. Consequently when Charles X of Sweden (1654–60) turned the tables on Denmark by his brilliant exploits in the war of 1657–8, totally defeated Christian IV's successor, Frederik III (1648–70), and forced him to cede the province of Scania, the last part of Sweden remaining in Danish hands, it was felt that the humiliation had been removed. Accordingly, in the Treaty of Roskilde, which brought the war to an end, the Frederiksborg set achieved an unusual honour for tapestries, a special mention in a stipulation, attached to the terms of peace, which provided that the offending tapestries should be covered over.[6]

Not long after, Christian V of Denmark undertook a sanguinary but inconclusive war against Sweden, the Scanian War (1675–9), in the fruitless hope of recovering the lost province. Both sides won various military successes, and the Danish King, imitating his grandfather and Louis XIV, commissioned tapestries to commemorate his victories, which were represented in a splendid series of panels intended for the decoration of the great hall in the Castle of Rosenborg.[7] These were executed in brilliant colours between 1684 and 1692 by the brothers Van der Eichen, Flemish weavers whom the King summoned to take charge of the tapestry looms established at Copenhagen, and were designed principally by Peder Andersen and Wilcken Ribolt. The seven military subjects show large figures of Christian V and other personages, with small-scale views of the actions and surrounding landscape in the background. They would appear to have been influenced by the conventional type of military tapestries evolved by the artists of Louis XIV, and consequently, in spite of the portraits and the landscapes, could hardly be called original in conception. The borders are adorned with trophies of banners, weapons, and drums, and have the Danish arms above with German inscriptions below.

6. *The Battle of Øland*, woven for Christian V of Denmark. Copenhagen, Rosenborg Castle.

The five naval subjects which illustrate the exploits of the famous Danish admiral, Niels Juel, are more original and show much more atmosphere and spirit, particularly those of the battles of Øland (Fig. 6)[8] and Køgebugt.

Three years after the completion of this Danish set, Charles XI of Sweden (1660–97), the opponent of Christian V in the Scanian War, accompanied by Tessin, his artistic adviser, visited his palace at Drottningholm, where the pictures by Lemke celebrating the King's victories over the Danes were hung.[9] Tessin, who doubtless was thinking of the Danish tapestries, suggested to the King that he should have some of Lemke's paintings reproduced in tapestry. Orders were given accordingly, but Charles XI died in 1697 and never saw the tapestries, which were executed at Beauvais by Béhagle and De la Croix, after cartoons by Martin based on Lemke's pictures, and only reached Sweden from 1699 onwards. In these noble panels with their rich fabric of gold, silk, and wool, the military operations are shown on an important scale, the foregrounds being taken up with horsemen in active conflict, corpses, and other details and battle

23

7. *The Siege of Malmö*, woven at Beauvais for Charles XI of Sweden. Swedish Royal Collection.

incidents to give a finish to the main strategic operations behind. The borders are of an architectural design, with columns and prisoners at the sides and an entablature along the top, broken by a large shield of arms supported by flying figures of Fame with trumpets. A cartouche below describes the subject of each in Latin: the second and third days of the *Battle of Lund*, the *Siege of Malmö* (Fig. 7), and the *Battle of Landskrona*. The tapestries are distinguished not only by their weaving and good composition, but especially by the charming tones of pink, blue, and brown, which show the famous Beauvais colouring at its best.

In England also, under Charles II (1660–85) and James II (1685–89), the example of Louis XIV was imitated by the tapestries of the *Battle of Solebay*, designed to illustrate the hard fought and indecisive naval battle off Southwold of the English and French fleets under the Duke of York, Lord Sandwich, and D'Estrées, against the Dutch under

De Ruyter in 1672.[10] Three sets of tapestries dealing with this event are known and they were woven by Francis and Thomas Poyntz[11] after cartoons which were probably designed by the Dutch artist William van de Velde. They belong to the later years of the Mortlake factory and some may even have been woven at Hatton Garden.

The largest and latest set consists of five panels, four of which bear the arms of George Legge, first Baron Dartmouth. This set was commissioned by James II in May 1688, no doubt for presentation to Lord Dartmouth, who had just assumed command of the fleet on the threat of a Dutch invasion. Before the end of the year, the Revolution had taken place and James II had been deposed, so that the tapestries never came into the possession of their intended owner. All the panels are framed by wide decorative borders filled with naval trophies, guns, rammers, globes, flags, lanterns, etc., and among them are flags bearing the crown and the cipher of James II.

The subjects are:

1. The allied fleets in line at dawn with the Dutch fleet appearing in the distance.

2. The rival fleets facing one another in line of battle.[12]

3. The fleets engaging with three ships burning furiously. One of these is perhaps the *Royal James*, Lord Sandwich's flagship which blew up with him and her crew.

4. The fleets drawing apart with four ships burning.[13]

5. An entrefenêtre with four British ships in the foreground and in the background other ships enveloped in flames and smoke.

Of these, the first, third, and fifth were in the collection of Mr. G. H. Lorimer[14] of Philadelphia, and the other two in that of Lord Iveagh. All but the fifth panel display the signature of Thomas Poyntz, who was the successor of Francis Poyntz and seems to have worked mainly in Hatton Garden, whither the Great Wardrobe removed in 1679. The tapestries bear the City of London shield, a variant of the Mortlake shield of St. George.

This most complete set is, as stated, probably later than the other two because it was presumably woven in 1688, whereas one of the other two, at Hampton Court, is signed by Francis Poyntz, who died in 1685. It is known that Francis Poyntz was at work on 'ten sea fights' in 1673. A note in the official Book of Petitions of 1678 states that he 'for twelve months had provided men to make a suite of sea fights and had made them so perfect in the work as could not be done without great expense and time'. Consequently all the existing tapestries can be dated within the comparatively narrow limits of 1673 and 1688. The third set is signed by Thomas Poyntz, but both the two earlier sets have fine decorative borders with amorini and dolphins, which present a much more pleasing appearance than the naval trophies of the Dartmouth set. The Hampton Court set consists of three panels. One is a replica of No. 1,[15] and another,[16] a new subject which can be called No. 6, represents the heat of the engagement, with the British ships hotly attacked by the Dutch, and seems to be an enlarged version of No. 5. The third panel is an entrefenêtre with ships burning and appears to be an excerpt from No. 3. The remaining set, which was also in Lord Iveagh's collection, bears the arms of Walpole, though it is not known what connection this family had with the battle in question. This consists of three panels, replicas of Nos. 2 and 3 and a slightly smaller version of No. 4.[17] All the Solebay tapestries are of extremely fine texture, thereby bringing out all the details of the rigging, bunting, and armament of the vessels, and the British ships fly the Union flag, which was adopted by the navy as a jack in 1607. The colouring throughout is soft and harmonious and admirably renders the distance and atmosphere of a seascape.

The Imperial House of Austria possessed a notable collection of military tapestries, now national property. Two sets[18] deal specifically with the campaigns of Archduke Charles V of Lorraine in the war against the Turks, whose investment of Vienna in 1683 so seriously threatened the dominions of the Hapsburgs. The earlier series, known as the *Victories of Duke Charles V*, was woven at Nancy about 1705 by Charles Mitté, and is marked with the double cross of Lorraine. It consists of five pieces, far removed in style from the courtly elegance of Van der Meulen's designs. *The Battle of Mohacs*, in particular, illustrates little more than a revolting group of headless and naked corpses piled round the edge of a pool, with some very conventional trees in the background. The later series, larger and in every way more important, was woven from designs by Charles

8. *The Battle of Kahlenberg*, one of the *Victories of Duke Charles V*. Vienna, Austrian State Collection.

9. *Military Life*, Flemish tapestry from a cartoon by Hyacinthe de la Peigne. Vienna, Austrian State Collection.

Herbel in the Archducal factory at La Malgrange from 1710 onwards and was begun by Mitté, although it was not completed until 1724. This set consists of no fewer than twenty-three subjects, in handsome caryatid and trophy borders, with a double shield of arms above and cartouche inscriptions below (Fig. 8). The draughtsmanship is good, and almost too pictorial for perfect representation by weaving. The principal characters, on horseback, occupy the foreground, as in Le Brun's designs, but instead of being merely ceremonial are engaged in active military movements and surrounded by fallen horses and the usual impedimenta of battle. In point of size, quality, and technique, this set ranks among the finest of its kind, and does not betray any evidence of its provincial origin.

A third Viennese series of a much later date consists merely of four scenes of military life in the field, a group of officers seated on the ground at an al fresco meal, a bivouac, troops in loose order with their families on the march, and so on. These were woven about the year 1740 in Brussels by Daniel Leyniers and Pierre van der Borcht, from cartoons by Hyacinthe de la Peigne.[19] They treat military life in rather an idyllic manner (Fig. 9), as might be expected in the age of Watteau, Boucher, and Casanova.

27

Such *fonctions militaires*, or the *Art of War*, as this group of subjects is generally called, can hardly be identified with any actual campaign, but belong to a well-known order of genre pictures such as any painter of military subjects might invent. They might, however, on occasion be used for a definite purpose and with little adaptation be made to serve as an illustration of a specific event; in fact, as we shall see, this had already been done in the case of an important series of military tapestries designed by the painter Lambert de Hondt.

CHAPTER IV

DE HONDT'S 'ART OF WAR' OF 1696

The 'Art of War': First Version (a)

WE have already noted how Louis XIV ordered rich sets of tapestries to perpetuate the memory of his victories in war and of his other achievements and how his example was followed by the Great Elector of Brandenburg, Christian V of Denmark, and Charles XI of Sweden. The Prussian and Danish monarchs, like Louis XIV, ordered their tapestries from looms established under French or Flemish weavers in their own dominions, but the Swedish set was obtained from Beauvais. Three other great military commanders of the later seventeenth century also desired to celebrate their prowess by sets of tapestries—the Elector Maximilian Emmanuel of Bavaria (1679–1726) (Fig. 53), the Margrave Louis of Baden (1677–1707), and William III of England (1689–1702). The first two wished to record their successes in the Turkish campaigns which followed the relief of Vienna in 1683 and culminated with the Elector's capture of Belgrade in 1688, and the last, his obstinate resistance to the grandiose schemes of Louis XIV himself. William III, however, did not patronize the weavers either of Holland or of Mortlake, but like the two German princes procured his tapestries in Brussels. Fortunately there is documentary evidence for the sets ordered by Maximilian Emmanuel and by William III (cf. App. IV, B).

The Munich Set

The information about the set ordered by the Elector Maximilian Emmanuel of Bavaria (which is known as the Munich Set) is especially complete and all the tapestries mentioned in the document, with one exception, can be identified beyond all doubt. The text runs thus:[1]

> *Achat par l'electeur Maximilien Emmanuel, le 1 avril*
> *1696, d'une suite de tapisseries de Bruxelles tissées par*
> *G. Van der Borcht et J. de Clercq.*
> *Mémorie* (sic) *des Tapisseries qui sont esté livrées le*
> *premier d'avril 1696 pour le service de S.A.E. par*
> *Jerosme De Clercq et Gaspar van der Borcht ambedeux*
> *Tapissiers de Sa d^{te} A.E.*

10. *Campement*, after L. de Hondt. Munich Set. Formerly Munich, Residenzmuseum, now Schleissheim, New Palace.

Les d^{tes} tapisseries consistantes en 8 pièces dont la première représente

1. *Le Campement de Cavallerie en une pièce de*	8	*aunes*
2. *Une autre pièce représentante l'action de la Cavallerie allante à faschines*	$6\frac{1}{4}$	
3. *Une Embuscade*	$9\frac{3}{4}$	
4. *Un Pillage*	$8\frac{1}{4}$	
5. *Une Marche*	9	
6. *Une pièce représentante le fouragement*	$9\frac{1}{4}$	
7. *Une Attacque*	$5\frac{1}{8}$	
8. *Rencontre*	$7\frac{1}{2}$	
	$63\frac{1}{8}$ a.	

Lesquelles multipliées par	6	*a. d'haut^r*
montent à	$378\frac{3}{4}$	
et à raison de	10 *escus p.a.*	
A la somme de	$3787\frac{1}{2}$ *escus*	

30

11. *Fachinade*, after L. de Hondt. Munich Set. Munich, Wittelsbacher Ausgleichsfonds.

This set still exists except for the last panel, *Rencontre*. There are wide borders of military trophies consisting of arms, armour, lances, bows, quivers, drums, trumpets, and saddles. In the centre of the lower borders there is an anvil which bears on its upper edge the title of the subject. The tapestries are, in the same order as the invoice:

1. *Campement* (Fig. 10). A camp scene outside a sutler's booth. At tables soldiers sit drinking, and smoking, and making love. In the centre stands a girl offering a cup of wine to a mounted dragoon, and a dismounted trooper tries to kiss her. A mounted trumpeter and a dismounted trooper leading his horse flank the group on either side. There is another sutler's booth in the middle distance on the left, and a mounted man rides towards the central group. The lower selvedge bears the Brussels mark and the name LE·CLERC.

2. *Fachinade* (Fig. 11). This shows a detachment of troopers on the outskirts of a wood, cutting brushwood and binding it into fascines. A noticeable motive is the horse represented with its head across the back of another. The lower selvedge has the Brussels mark and the name LE·CLERC.

31

12. *Embuscade*, after L. de Hondt. Munich Set. Formerly Munich, Residenzmuseum, now Schleissheim, New Palace.

3. *Embuscade* (Fig. 12). A convoy with its mounted escort has been surprised by infantry hidden in woods on either side of a defile. The convoy tries to escape at a gallop while the escort gallantly engages the enemy ambush at point-blank range. In the foreground a trooper and his horse have fallen together just under the feet of the officer in command, who, sword in hand, is trying to restore order and rescue his charge. In the centre of the foreground is the artist's signature L. DE HONDT. INV. ET PINX. Although the new photograph used for Fig. 12 shows the *Embuscade* with a correct Munich border, this border was missing from a photograph taken in the 1930s (cf. description of *La Halte*, p. 92). The lower selvedge has the Brussels mark and signature LE·CLERC.

4. *Pillage* (Fig. 13). A detachment of mounted men is raiding a village. On the left some of the party are driving off pigs, sheep, and cattle, while on the right others, dismounted, are beating or binding peasant men and women. One is even searching the pockets of a peasant who has fallen prostrate and senseless. In the middle distance on the right a man is throwing bundles from the gable window of a cottage,

14. *La Marche*, after L. de Hondt. Munich Set.
Formerly Munich, National Museum.
Schleissheim, New Palace (?).

13. *Pillage*, after L. de Hondt. Munich Set. Formerly Munich, Residenzmuseum, now stored in the Palace of Nymphenburg.

and smoke and flames are already rising from the thatch of another cottage in the centre. In the lower left hand corner is the artist's signature L. DE HONDT INV. &. PINX. As with *Embuscade* (above) the new photograph used for Fig. 13 shows a correct Munich border, although this border does not appear in a photograph taken in the 1930s (cf. description of *La Halte*, p. 92). The lower selvedge has the Brussels mark and signature LE·CLERC.

5. *La Marche* (Fig. 14). On the left the Commander-in-Chief, carrying his baton, is riding with his staff from the shade of a group of trees towards the centre. The Commander, whose features seem definitely intended as a portrait of the Elector Maximilian Emmanuel (Fig. 53), is preceded by two runners or guides on foot. Before the Commander ride two trumpeters and a drummer, who wear the Bavarian colours, and on the drum are the Wittelsbach arms. A mounted body-guard rides ahead of all. In the right hand front corner, several peasant women, with their babies and other belongings, sit on the ground and watch the army pass. In the background the whole force is seen to be on the move. On the lower selvedge is the Brussels mark and the name LE·CLERC.

6. *Fouragement* (Fig. 15). A wide landscape is occupied by a large party of soldiers, mounted and on foot, engaged in cutting forage and carting it away in wagons, or tying it into bundles to be loaded onto the backs of their horses. Two men binding trusses of grass are prominent in the foreground, and a lamb with its legs tied lies on the ground between them. These men are directed by another, who stands with a scythe over his left shoulder under a tree. To the left is a party of mounted men and led horses. The lower selvedge bears the Brussels mark and the signature A CASTRO.*

7. *Attacque* (Fig. 16). In the foreground, mounted troopers with the help of dismounted men are loading fascines on their saddle-bows. On the left, a column of

* Editorial Note. Jacob van der Borcht (who was privileged in 1676) and his son Jasper (Gaspar), are known to have operated, in association with Jerome Le Clerc, an important tapestry business in Brussels in the period between 1676 and 1742 (see Göbel, *Wandteppiche*, vol. 1, p. 396 f.). Göbel explains the signature A CASTRO (A C) as being used by Jasper (Gaspar) to avoid confusion with his father's signature during the period of about ten years when they worked together, before the father's retirement. Our first definitive date for Jasper's work as a full member of the firm is from the existing French document (p. 29) of memorandum and invoice of the Munich Set, delivered in April 1696, under the proprietary names of 'Jerosme De Clercq et Gaspar van der Borcht ambedeux Tapissiers'. Göbel says that the father was still working in the middle of the first decade of the eighteenth century. This would carry a minimum ten year period of joint activity to about 1706. It is worthy of note that the proportion of signatures on the seven Munich panels is five for Le Clerc and two for A Castro. The signature on the Blenheim Palace *Rencontre* panel, dated 1706, is Le Clerc. It is to the period of joint activity of father and son that Dr. Eva Zimmermann assigns the Karlsruhe cycle (the Baden Set).

15. *Fouragement*, after L. de Hondt. Munich Set. Formerly Munich, National Museum. Schleissheim, New Palace (?).

16. *Attacque*, after L. de Hondt. Munich Set. Munich, Wittelsbacher Ausgleichsfonds.

troopers with fascines already loaded rides into the distance towards a walled town on a hill, the siege of which is already in progress. In the town is a large church or cathedral with a tall spire. In the lower left hand corner is the artist's signature L. D. HONDT. INV. ET. PINXIT. The lower selvedge bears the Brussels mark and the signature A CASTRO.

To these seven we can add a description of the eighth panel, which is now missing, from the corresponding tapestry (now in Karlsruhe) of the contemporary Baden Set (Fig. 21), q.v.

> 8. *Rencontre*. In the centre and right foreground is a confused mêlée of two bodies of cavalry hotly engaged round a standard bearing the device of a mailed arm holding a sword. This resembles the Polish royal flag.[2] The man who carries this standard is being thrust through with a sabre by a dragoon, who is being attacked in his turn by another. On the right a dismounted trooper is trying to raise his horse, which has fallen, and on the left another dragoon and his horse have fallen together. In the middle distance, by a group of trees, other bodies of horse are seen charging each other, and in the background on the left is a town on a hill.

Of the seven surviving panels of this set, two (*Fachinade* and *Attacque*) were formerly owned by Crown Prince Rupprecht of Bavaria (cf. p. 92), three (*Campement, Embuscade,* and *Pillage*) were in the Residenzmuseum in Munich, and two (*La Marche* and *Fourage-ment*) were in the National Museum in Munich.* Certain panels of the Munich Set, notably those from the Residenzmuseum, are now being rearranged in the New Palace at Schleissheim, the palace which the Elector Maximilian Emmanuel built for himself near Munich at the beginning of the eighteenth century (see p. 102n).

It will be recognized that the panels of the Munich Set all illustrate not particular events but everyday incidents of military life on active service, and that only one, *La Marche*, gives an opportunity for glorifying the Commander-in-Chief and his staff. Although they were apparently ordered to commemorate the Elector's successes in the Turkish War, none of the tapestries seems to refer to it or indeed to military operations in south-eastern Europe. Some of the arms of the trophies in the borders, the bows and quivers for instance, alone suggest contact with Turkish troops. Otherwise the landscapes and costumes rather suggest the cockpit of Europe or the Rhine country.

Two small tapestries of entrefenêtre shape (Figs. 17, 18) have long been hung at Schleissheim with another but later set of about 1724, which is known as the Schleissheim Set (see p. 97 and Figs. 54–67). These two panels differ from the Schleissheim Set, however, not only in style and execution, but also in the borders, which are those of

* Editorial Note. *Fachinade* and *Attacque* are now owned by the Wittelsbacher Ausgleichsfonds, a foundation to which the late Crown Prince Rupprecht donated much of his collection.

17. *A mounted trooper questioning a peasant.*
    Schleissheim, New Palace.

18. *A forager whipping up his horse.*
    Schleissheim, New Palace.

the Munich Set. Although these two panels are not mentioned in the invoice quoted above, the existence of part of the border of a duplicate *Campement* suggests that some additional pieces were obtained to supplement the Munich Set. In the lower borders there are anvils unfortunately uninscribed. One piece (Fig. 17) shows two mounted troopers, one of them questioning a standing peasant, the other refreshing himself by drinking from a large jug. In the foreground a soldier seated on a log smokes a long pipe, and in the background, tents and other mounted men are to be seen. The second piece (Fig. 18) shows in the background the spires and towers of a town, and in the middle distance are mounted men and a group of tents. In the foreground a soldier standing on a rock tries to mount his horse, which, already loaded on either side with hay, is disinclined to carry its master as well. Against the rock leans a scythe. The former could well serve as an adjunct to the *Campement* and the latter to the *Fouragement* scene.

19. *The Battle of Belgrade*, possibly woven at Brussels.

One other panel representing a military subject (Fig. 19)[3] has exactly the same borders as the Munich Set, but unfortunately the anvil is uninscribed so that there is no title for the subject. On the right the Commander-in-Chief and his staff, all mounted, stand by a clump of trees and watch the progress of a battle in the background. A coloured orderly gallops towards them from the left. The landscape has a more eastern character than the De Hondt designs just described, and the appearance of the city and the geographical details suggest that the *Battle of Belgrade* in 1688 may here be represented. To judge by the photograph (for we have not been able to see the original) the tapestry is of Brussels workmanship from the looms of either Van der Borcht or Le Clerc, but does not seem to have been woven after a cartoon by De Hondt. The figures are clumsier and the horses heavier than in his drawings, and the treatment of the whole scene considerably coarser.

The Baden Set

The Grand-Ducal collection of Baden[4] possessed a set of six tapestries from De Hondt's designs, woven by Le Clerc and Van der Borcht, which is generally believed, though definite evidence is lacking, to have belonged to the Margrave Louis of Baden, well known as the 'Türkensieger'.[5] He was a colleague of the Elector in the Turkish War, but later, as an ally of Marlborough, fought against him in the War of the Spanish Succession. Each of the six panels bears its title on an anvil in the lower border. They are:

> *Campement* (Fig. 20).
>
> *Fachinade.*
>
> *Embuscade*, which has the signature L. D. HONDT and, in the selvedge, I · V · D · BORCHT A CASTRO.
>
> *Pillage.*
>
> *Attacque*, with the signature of L. D. HONDT.
>
> *Rencontre* (Fig. 21).

The *Campement, Fachinade*[6] and *Rencontre* panels are now in the Badisches Landesmuseum, Karlsruhe. They apparently have no signatures.

The subjects and the borders are generally the same as those of the Munich Set, but the borders display one striking difference. At the bottom of the side borders there are, so to speak, supporters in the persons of full-length figures of soldiers. In four of the panels the figures are the same, a musketeer on the left and a trooper on the right, but in the other two, *Campement* and *Pillage*, the supporters are varied to suit the subjects. *Campement* has on the left a soldier carrying a basket of provisions on his shoulder and

20. *Campement*, after L. de Hondt. Baden Set. Karlsruhe, Badisches Landesmuseum.

on the right a trumpeter in the act of sounding. *Pillage* has on the left a musketeer laden with loot in the form of large jugs and on the right a trooper carrying a bundle of fodder on his back.

The William III Set

Wauters[7] quotes a document dated June 15th, 1700, which indicates that William III of England procured a quantity of tapestry from Brussels through his agent, the artist Lottin. Three complete sets are mentioned and one is called *d'Exercitie van den Oorloghe*, *The Art of War*, after the designs of De Hondt. The date of this set is so close to that of the De Hondt tapestries supplied to the Elector Maximilian Emmanuel that there is every reason to believe that it comprised some, if not all, of the same eight subjects,

40

21. *Rencontre*, after L. de Hondt. Baden Set. Karlsruhe, Badisches Landesmuseum.

but unfortunately it cannot now be identified. At the same time, William III ordered, also through Lottin, three special tapestries to commemorate his own personal successes, the *Battle of Bresgate*, the *Landing at Torbay*, and the *Battle of the Boyne*.[8] These were to be woven by Le Clerc, De Vos, Van der Borcht, and Cobus, but there is no evidence that they were completed or that, if woven, they are still in existence. These two sets, if they could be traced, would most certainly provide important fresh material.[9]

Part of a set of tapestries woven after these designs of De Hondt was formerly in the possession of M. Founès of Paris (see also p. 108, X). There are three panels only, without borders, *Campement* (an incomplete panel, the right half only), *La Marche*, and *Rencontre*.[10] They are well woven and may possibly be William III's set (see App. IV, B), sold on the expulsion of the House of Orange in 1799. In *La Marche* there are some slight differences

41

in the features and dress of the Commander-in-Chief and his staff, but they are not sufficient to suggest that this tapestry was intended to portray another general quite different from the hero of the Munich panel (Fig. 53). There are no Wittelsbach arms. In these generalized campaign scenes the Brussels weavers, shrewd men of business, would hardly have troubled to give an exact portrait of the patron who had ordered the set, even in the one subject which provided an opportunity for depicting the Commander-in-Chief. All they could be expected to do would be to produce a conventional portrait of a contemporary general with such composite features that he could be recognized as Maximilian Emmanuel, William III, Louis of Baden, Turenne, or even Louis XIV, with equal probability, according to the taste of the purchaser.

The Lisbon Set

There is another set of the first version of the *Art of War* tapestries in the Museum in Lisbon. Arms of four lilies appear on them. There are four pieces—*Fachinade*, *Pillage*, *La Marche*, and *Rencontre*.[11]

These sets of tapestries are of considerable importance in giving a clue to the basis for the designs of a long series of later military tapestries woven to commemorate the War of the Spanish Succession, such as the Blenheim Palace 'Victories' (see Chapter VI) made for the great Duke of Marlborough (1650–1722), or the Schleissheim Set (see p. 90 ff.) made for his opponent Maximilian Emmanuel. It has hitherto been assumed that Van der Meulen, who died in 1690, was, if not the actual artist of them, at least the master of the artist; and this, as we shall see below, has caused several of these panels to be assigned to an earlier date than is possible. In the following chapters these various tapestries will be described and grouped, and it is hoped to show that, as they can all be connected with the War of the Spanish Succession, which began in 1702, Van der Meulen cannot have designed any of them, but that on the contrary they are stylistically related to the military set of the *Art of War*, or *fonctions militaires*, by Lambert de Hondt, and that he and his school must rather be regarded as the source of inspiration for the cartoons.

CHAPTER V

MARLBOROUGH AND HIS GENERALS

WHEN Blenheim and Ramillies and the other brilliant victories of the Allies in the War of the Spanish Succession had ruined the prestige of the French army and the tradition that it was invincible, it was only natural for Marlborough (Fig. 39), Prince Eugene, and the other Allied generals to commemorate their exploits with battle paintings and tapestries. The use of tapestries to celebrate victories over France turned one of the weapons of Louis XIV against himself, so to speak, since he had glorified his own military achievements in the tapestries of the *Histoire du Roi* and the Elector Maximilian Emmanuel too had recorded his own prowess by tapestries. It was thus highly suitable that the Duke should hang the great palace which Vanbrugh was erecting for him at Woodstock with tapestries depicting his victories. In 1709 Sir Richard Blackmore, in his poem 'Instructions to Vanderbank', criticized in the *Tatler* of that year, urged the Flemish weaver, then in charge of looms in London, to produce for the new Palace of Blenheim tapestries worthy of the hero and his deeds. It begins:

> *Not one rich genius left that can sustain*
> *Th' expensive Task of Marlbro's last campaign:*
> *Ruin'd by Conquests, do they pray for peace*
> *That the hard Taxes on the Muse may cease?*
> *Thou, Artist, who dost Nature's face express*
> *In silk and gold, and scenes of Action dress;*
> *Dost figured Arras animated leave,*
> *Spin a bright Story or a Passion weave*
> *By mingling threads, canst mingle shades and light,*
> *Delineate Triumphs or describe a fight;*
> *Do thou relate the Hero's toil, record*
> *The new Achievement of his matchless sword.*
> *Belgian, attend, and from thy noble Loom*
> *Let the great Chief, August in Triumph come.*
> *For Blenheim's lofty Rooms the work design,*
> *In every Piece let Art and Labour shine:*
> *Let glorious Deeds the Briton's Palace crown,*
> *Not those of ancient Heroes, but his own.*
> *In that bright Series of thy Story show*
> *What Albion, what Mankind, to Marlbro owe.*

43

The Duke of Marlborough, however, and those of his generals who followed his example did not patronize English looms but turned to those of Flanders, which the exploits of Marlborough's troops had wrested from France.

At Blenheim Palace there are two sets of military tapestries which bear the arms of John Churchill, the great Duke of Marlborough, and though no exact record of their acquisition seems to have been preserved in the inventories or archives of the palace, he must presumably have acquired them either by gift or by purchase.

The 'Art of War': First Version (b)

The First Blenheim Palace Set (c. 1706)

The first Blenheim Palace set consists of five panels which repeat in whole or in part some of the subjects of the *Art of War* by De Hondt. This set was woven by Le Clerc and Van der Borcht and is of excellent quality.

> *Campement* (Fig. 22) bears the Brussels mark BB and AC (for A CASTRO, i.e. Van der Borcht, see note on p. 34).
>
> *Pillage*, centre, and *Pillage*, right (Figs. 23, 24). Two separate pieces for entrefenêtres.
>
> *Attacque* (Fig. 25).
>
> *Rencontre* (Fig. 26) bears the Brussels mark BB and the name and date LE CLERC 1706. There is no evidence whether this is the date of the order or of the delivery.

The *Campement*, *Attacque*, and *Rencontre* panels all have wide borders of military trophies with the Churchill arms in the centre at the top and in the middle of the lower border a pile of plate, a mortar, and a trophy of colours. They are in the Bow Window Room. The two *Pillage* panels, which are in the Third State Room, have borders at the top and bottom only, but like the others have the Churchill arms in the centre of the top border. In this set, however, there are no medallions of Virtues in the four angles as in the 'Victories', to which we shall come later (p. 60). There is a considerable amount of gold woven in the tapestries in a heavy manner resembling basket-work (see App. IV, C). This first set, which alone of the tapestries at Blenheim Palace with the arms of the great Duke is heavily worked with gold, may have been presented to him on some famous occasion, possibly as a gift of which he might have supervised the execution. It may have been a gift from the city of Brussels on his state entry into that city on May 28th, 1706, after the victory of Ramillies, which drove the French out of Flanders. Such a set of the *Art of War* would have been a graceful tribute to the victorious commander. It was a tradition in Brussels to offer sets of tapestry to a visiting sovereign, to a new

22. *Campement*, after L. de Hondt. First Blenheim Palace Set. Blenheim Palace, Duke of Marlborough.

25. *Attacque*, after L. de Hondt. First Blenheim Palace Set. Blenheim Palace, Duke of Marlborough.

23, 24. *Pillage* (centre and right portions), after L. de Hondt.
    First Blenheim Palace Set. Blenheim Palace, Duke of Marlborough.

26. *Rencontre*, after L. de Hondt. First Blenheim Palace Set. Blenheim Palace, Duke of Marlborough.

viceroy, or to any similar person of high importance.[1] The Churchill arms on the set show that he was already a Prince of the Holy Roman Empire, so that the tapestries must date after 1704.*

* Editorial Note. The fact that the designs, as will be seen below, do not show the same variations from the original sets (Munich and Baden) as do those of the Generals lends credence to the theory that the Blenheim Palace *Art of War* may be earlier than those of the Generals, a theory which the date (1706) on the *Rencontre* would support. Certain of the variations to be found in the Generals' sets, even,

48

This first Blenheim Palace set is alluded to by Seeley in the second edition of his account of Stowe (published in 1797) and he says:

'The State Dressing Room, hung with tapestry, worked by a subscription of Lord Cobham and other officers serving under the Duke of Marlborough; it represents the functions of the cavalry in the army of the Allies:—The great piece represents part of the Battle of Wynendael Wood. Similar sets were worked for

the Duke of Marlborough, at Blenheim;
Lord Cadogan, at Caversham;
the Duke of Argyle, at Inverary;
Lord Orkney, at Clifden
General Lumly, at Stanstead;
and for General Webb.'

The 'Art of War' : First Version (c)

The six sets woven for Marlborough's Generals

Three of these sets can no longer be traced.

The Cadogan Set presumably perished in the fire at Caversham in the eighteenth century.

The set belonging to the second Duke of Argyll (Marlborough's friend), who left his possessions to his four daughters, cannot now be traced, and no knowledge of it exists in the family.

At Biddesden there is no record of any tapestries made for General Webb, although a large equestrian portrait of that tough old warrior, of whom Thackeray made so much in *Henry Esmond* for family reasons, still hangs in the hall and shows the Battle of Wynendael as a background, with a plan of the action in one corner.

The remaining three sets can be identified.

From Lord Orkney's set, three panels with his arms at the top are still at Cliveden, having been in the possession of the late Viscount Astor. These are said to have been purchased in Paris by the first Viscount Astor. They are now the property of the National Trust.

seem to bear a closer connection with the original Munich and Baden sets than do the Blenheim Palace examples. In the baffling problem of dating the sets ordered individually by Marlborough's Generals there are other important considerations to be taken into account, such as the individual taste of the patron as well as his own problems of space, the technical weaving problems, and the choice of a suitable occasion to commemorate, quite apart from the reasonable assumption that the Generals were following an example initiated by their Commander-in-Chief.

49

27. *Campement,* after L. de Hondt. Orkney Set. Cliveden, formerly Viscount Astor, now Property of the National Trust.

28. *Attacque*, after L. de Hondt. Orkney Set. Cliveden, formerly Viscount Astor, now Property of the National Trust.

Campement (Fig. 27). This panel roughly corresponds with the left half of the Munich panel. A new figure, however, is introduced in the left foreground of a soldier smoking a pipe, and the mounted man in the background does not appear.

Embuscade, showing roughly the left central part of the Munich panel.

Attacque (Fig. 28).

La Marche, a fourth panel, is at Brown University, in Providence, Rhode Island.*

Lord Cobham's set at Stowe was sold and dispersed at the sale of the contents of Stowe in July, 1921.[2] It consisted of:

Campement (Fig. 29), popularly called 'The Poisoning of the Spy'. This panel shows approximately the central third of the Munich tapestry, but the figure of the seated soldier, smoking a pipe, which appears in the Cliveden panel is placed in front of the left-hand horse. The mounted man and the two men with muskets in the background do not appear.

Embuscade, popularly called 'Wynendael', and signed A CASTRO. It has been slightly altered in the left foreground.†

Fouragement. The white horse in the centre is wearing a saddle-cloth fastened by a girth. These do not appear in the Munich panel, of which this shows only a part.

Attacque, popularly called the 'Burning of Lille'.[3] This is practically the same as the Munich panel.

Both *Campement* and *Attacque* have the factory marks and weaver's initials L C. *Campement* and *Fouragement* were at one time in the house of Mrs. James J. Preston of Wilton Place, Beaconsfield. *Campement* and *Attacque* were sold at Sotheby's in 1963.[4]

* The existence of this panel was reported in 1943 by Miss Gertrude Townsend of the Boston Museum of Fine Arts and identified with her help. The late Duke of Hamilton, in a letter to Dr. Wriston, then President of Brown University, thus identified the arms: 'The Lord Lyon King of Arms tells me that the arms shown are those "usurped and assumed unto himself" by the celebrated General, the Earl of Orkney, K.T.—but which have never been matriculated in Lyon Register, so the tapestries were evidently made for him. You will recall that this Earl of Orkney was one of Marlborough's most prominent generals, and younger brother to the Fourth Duke of Hamilton.'

[Editorial note: The author saw the panel in Providence in 1954 and confirmed his opinion which he had previously noted thus: 'It is clear that the Providence tapestry is a panel of the Orkney set which has strayed away from its fellows. It is one of the revised versions of the *first* edition of the "Art of War" which were woven for Marlborough and his generals and one or two others at the beginning of the eighteenth century. The *second* edition as represented by the Schleissheim and other sets is later.']

† An *Embuscade* panel in the possession of Viscount Bearsted has been on exhibition at the Birmingham Museum and Art Gallery since 1947, as 'one of a series of eight tapestries called the "Art of War" from cartoons by Lambert de Hondt. Flemish, Brussels, ca. 1700. Mark BB. A. Castro.' As the arms have been identified as those of Temple of Stowe the panel would appear to belong to the original Cobham Set from Stowe.

29. *Campement*, after L. de Hondt. Cobham Set. Formerly at Stowe.

The Lumley Set was perhaps brought to England by Richard Lumley, 1st Earl of Scarbrough, who had rebuilt Stansted in 1687, or by his eldest son.[5] The set is larger than any of the others and consists of nine panels derived from seven of the eight original subjects of the Munich Set. The subjects depicted are:

Campement (Fig. 34), lengthened on the left and right and with a new scene of a seated group of officers on the right.

30. *Fachinade*, after L. de Hondt. Lumley Set. Stansted Park, Earl of Bessborough.

31. *Embuscade*, after L. de Hondt. Lumley Set. Stansted Park, Earl of Bessborough.

32. *Pillage* (left portion), after L. de Hondt. Lumley Set. West Berlin, Bodenheim.

33. *Pillage* (right portion), after L. de Hondt. Lumley Set. Formerly London, Leopold Albu.

34. *Campement*, after L. de Hondt. Lumley Set. Stansted Park, Earl of Bessborough.

35. *La Marche*, after L. de Hondt. Lumley Set. Formerly London, Leopold Albu.

36. *Fouragement* (centre portion), after L. de Hondt. Lumley Set. London, J. Benardout.

37. *Fouragement* (right portion), after L. de Hondt. Lumley Set. West Berlin, Bodenheim.

Fachinade (Fig. 30), somewhat altered from the original Munich panel, having a man wielding an axe on the left instead of the group chopping up branches.

Embuscade (Fig. 31), lengthened on the right.

Pillage (Fig. 32), left half.

Pillage (Fig. 33), right half.

La Marche (Fig. 35), left portion. The horses follow the original design, but the riders are in armour instead of in uniform, and the features of the Commander-in-Chief resemble those of the Duke of Marlborough.

Fouragement (Fig. 36), the centre, with the lamb with its legs tied, slightly altered.

Fouragement (Fig. 37), the right portion, considerably altered.

57

38. *Rencontre*, after L. de Hondt. Lumley Set.
Formerly London, Leopold Albu.

Rencontre (Fig. 38), the left and central portions, signed L·C· for Le Clerc and with the Brussels mark.

The Lumley Set was sold at Christie's on May 18th, 1911, and came into the possession of Mr. Leopold Albu. At Mr. Albu's death the tapestries were sold again at Christie's on May 19th, 1938. The *Embuscade* panel was bought by the late Earl of Bessborough for Stansted Park and the remaining panels by Count Edward Raczynski, who sold them at Sotheby's on October 13th, 1961. At this sale the present Lord Bessborough bought the *Campement* and *Fachinade* panels, so that these, with the *Embuscade* panel, are now restored to their original home, Stansted Park. Of the others

58

the *Pillage* (left portion) and *Fouragement* (right portion) are now in the possession of Bodenheim of West Berlin, and the *Fouragement* (centre portion) was bought by J. Benardout.

Except for the Orkney Set, which has trophy borders like the set at Blenheim Palace, all the existing sets made for Marlborough's Generals have picture-frame borders of the type which became popular in the eighteenth century, with the coats of arms inserted in the centre of the top border. This fashion was introduced at the Gobelins and copied at Brussels and other tapestry centres. The rich trophy borders of the Blenheim and Orkney sets are really a survival from the previous century.

The panels of the Blenheim Palace, Cobham, Orkney, and Lumley sets were all woven, as we have seen, after the original designs of Lambert de Hondt for the Munich Set made by Le Clerc and Van der Borcht for the Elector Maximilian Emmanuel in 1696. They were also all woven, so far as the weavers' marks exist, by the same firm, whereas the 'Victories' of the Duke of Marlborough and the later military tapestries made for the Elector Maximilian Emmanuel at Schleissheim, Augustus the Strong, and other patrons, were all woven by Judocus de Vos. This seems to imply that Lambert de Hondt's original *Art of War* cartoons had remained the property of Le Clerc and Van der Borcht, who could still use them or adapt them for other sets, and that as a result De Vos had to work from fresh designs when he received the later commissions. It was quite usual for the cartoons to remain in the weaver's possession.

The Blenheim Palace set of the *Art of War* differs somewhat from the three surviving sets woven for Marlborough's Generals in its variations from the original Munich and Baden sets. The balance of the evidence at present known, taking into consideration as well other than merely pictorial arguments, seems to support the theory that the Blenheim Palace set precedes those of Marlborough's Generals, though the whole period is a comparatively short one. Since some of the variations, particularly in the Generals' sets, form links, as will be seen, with the later sets woven by De Vos for the Elector Maximilian Emmanuel for Schleissheim and for Augustus the Strong, it is probable, as already proposed, that the Blenheim Palace set ante-dates the other three. If the Blenheim Palace set was woven after Ramillies in 1706, as a gift of the City of Brussels (see p. 44), then the Cobham, Orkney, and Lumley sets may perhaps have been ordered either during the remaining hostilities or after their conclusion.

CHAPTER VI

THE BLENHEIM PALACE 'VICTORIES'

JOHN CHURCHILL, Duke of Marlborough (Fig. 39), desiring yet another set of tapestries to adorn his new palace of Blenheim* and this time to commemorate and represent the actual events of his victorious campaigns, did not have recourse to the weavers of his own country, who had gradually dispersed about London after the close of the Mortlake factory and the establishment of the Great Wardrobe (about 1680). Instead, as before, he sought those of the province in which he had for years been more or less continuously engaged. The Brussels looms were still flourishing after an uninterrupted career of over two centuries and the craftsman he selected for his purpose was the well known Judocus or Josse de Vos, the weaver of the famous Alexander series at Hampton Court (see App. IV, II).

At the time that these tapestries were put in hand, De Vos may have been actually engaged upon the important commission from the Austrian Emperor to reproduce the *Conquest of Tunis* series from the Vermeyen cartoons at Brussels (see p. 14). His loom capacity must have been considerable, for in addition to the Duke of Marlborough's order he was able to undertake commissions of a similar nature for several other patrons (see pp. 102-11), most of which were completed between 1712 and 1724.[1]

The Blenheim Palace 'Victories' alone consist of ten large panels† illustrating Marlborough's principal victories with the single exception of Ramillies. They hang in the three main state rooms of the palace and in an inner room adjoining the apartments of the Duke and Duchess.

Taken in their chronological order, with the names of the rooms in which they are hung, the subjects are as follows, the titles given in the borders not always being those by which we know them:

1. *Dunawert* (Donauwörth), July 2, 1704 (Fig. 40). First State Room.
2. *Hooghstet* (Blenheim), August 13, 1704 (Fig. 42). Green Writing-room.
3. *Forcing the Lines of Brabant* (no title), July 18, 1705 (Fig. 43). First State Room.
4. *Aldenarda* (Oudenarde), July 11, 1708 (Fig. 45). Third State Room.
5. *Wynendael*, September 28, 1708 (Fig. 46). Green Writing-room.

---

* For Marlborough House he chose a series of wall-paintings by Laguerre, which are still there and have been engraved.

† The first five are reproduced in the first edition of Churchill's *Marlborough: His Life and Times*, vol. II, pp. 386, 452, 568; vol. III, pp. 408, 512.

39. Kneller: *John Churchill, 1st Duke of Marlborough*. Oil. Blenheim Palace, Duke of Marlborough.

6. *Insulae* (Surrender of Lille), December 9, 1708 (Fig. 47). First State Room.

7. *Montes Hannoniae* (Malplaquet), September 11, 1709 (Fig. 48). First State Room.

8. *Bouchain I*, September 13, 1711 (Fig. 50). Second State Room.

9. *Bouchain II* (Fig. 49). Third State Room.

10. *Bouchain III* (Fig. 51). Second State Room.

The panels are roughly 14 feet 6 inches in height, enclosed in wide and handsome trophy borders, which recall those of the 1696 Munich and Baden sets of De Hondt's *Art of War* (Figs. 10–16, 20, 21). They have, however, been specially designed for the occasion, with gold-coloured medallions containing allegorical figures of the Virtues in the four corners, with a Pegasus and a thunderbolt in the central cartouches at the sides. A distinctive feature of the design is a large mortar, or pile of plate or accoutrements, projecting from the middle of the lower border into the foreground of the picture. The central ornament at the top consists of an oval medallion charged with the emblem or arms of the place represented—a tower for Bouchain, a fleur-de-lis for Lille, and so on—with a label below bearing its Latin name. There being no such name available for the 'Lines of Brabant', this medallion bears the Churchill arms instead, as in the first set.

The widths are not all alike, two of the Bouchain panels and the Blenheim panel being about 25 feet wide, and the others about half this width. The weaver's name occurs on four of the panels in the blue selvedge, which has been turned back, and is missing in others, owing to the selvedge having been cut away. The figure-drawing, horses, and landscapes are of a high order of artistic merit; and the weaving, especially the colouring, is up to the best standard of Brussels eighteenth-century work, and practically equivalent to that of the Gobelins.

No exact record has been found to throw light on the circumstances in which the commission for the tapestries was given. They may have been ordered by the Duke himself, or possibly they were among his many gifts of honour. The tapestries cannot all have been woven before 1711 because Bouchain was not taken until September of that year. Consequently it is possible that they were not ordered until 1712, the year when Marlborough left England to spend some two years abroad more or less in exile.* The misfortunes (including the loss of Bouchain) which had befallen the Allies in Flanders in the campaign of 1712 being then quite recent, events might certainly have suggested to the Duke that his last brilliant success in the field, the capture of Bouchain from the French under the eyes of Villars and a superior force in 1711, should be commemorated with three tapestries to emphasize the failures of his successor.

The cartoons, if stylistic likenesses are any criterion, were probably designed by the school of the author of the *Art of War* of 1696, that is to say by Lambert de Hondt or his pupils. Great care has been taken throughout in the accurate depicting of the military operations and in the topography, and these details agree with the plans given by Coxe and those found in other works more or less contemporary. The uniforms and equipment as well as the movements of the troops are also well rendered and the artist must have been a keen observer of military tactics and manœuvres. The portraiture so far as concerns those who are clearly recognizable—Marlborough, Boufflers, and Colonel Armstrong—is reasonably good, and it is possible that if good named portraits of other members of Marlborough's staff were available, more of them could be identified.†

* David Green, however, suggests that the first 'Victories' may have been ordered before the siege of Bouchain and the three Bouchain tapestries added later (see App. IV, D, E, F, G).

† We have, unfortunately, not been able to obtain a photograph of the picture at Culford Hall which shows Marlborough, Cadogan, and other officers.

The events leading up to what is known as 'The War of the Spanish Succession' arose directly out of the death without an heir of Charles II of Spain, on November 1st, 1700. The situation, naturally, had not been unanticipated. It had formed the subject of a Treaty of Partition as early as 1698, but since then it had remained a bone of contention between the aged Emperor Leopold of Austria and Louis XIV of France, both of whom put forward claimants to the throne with about equal rights of succession. The sympathies of Europe favoured the claim of the Emperor rather than that of Louis, whose schemes of self-aggrandizement were a universal cause of alarm; but Louis had so forestalled the issue as to get his candidate, Philip, Duke of Anjou, second son of the Dauphin, nominated by the dying King as his successor, and actually accepted by the Spanish nation under the title of Philip V. The matter, however, was not to be allowed to rest there. The Dutch, supported by William III, were strongly opposed to the Treaty of Ryswick, only recently concluded by him with France, and Leopold was ready to go to war once more on behalf of the imperial candidate, the Archduke Charles.

The first overt move in the new hostilities was made by Louis, who dispatched a force to resume his hold on the Dutch frontier towns and at the same time entered into active co-operation with his ally, the Elector of Bavaria, who had been governor of the Spanish Netherlands from 1692 until 1699 and had put forward his son Joseph Ferdinand before his premature death in 1699 as a candidate for the Spanish throne. Louis nevertheless consented to open negotiations at The Hague, whither William III himself, hoping to gain time while he strengthened his position elsewhere, had gone on July 3rd, 1701. The Emperor was hampered by a rising rebellion in Hungary and by fresh threats of a Turkish invasion, and was by no means in a favourable condition for taking the field. He was able, however, to make a counter-move by sending an army under Prince Eugene of Savoy into Italy, where the French hold was vulnerable and precarious.

The part played by the English King at this juncture was a very difficult one, with a Tory Government strongly against him, and Marlborough, whom he had taken with him to Holland as negotiator, more than suspected of personal disaffection. The latter, however, threw himself energetically into the preparations for war, and set about enlarging the Grand Alliance by entering into treaties of support with Denmark, Sweden, and the Elector Frederick of Brandenburg, who was to be recognized as King of Prussia. The Hague negotiations he treated from the outset as illusory.

Such was the state of affairs when, on September 16th, 1701, the death of the exiled James II, and the proclamation of his son (the Old Pretender) as King by Louis XIV, threw the whole weight of popular feeling in England into the scales against France, and precipitated the declaration of war. The death of William III on March 8th, 1702, and the accession of Anne, who was Marlborough's devoted patron, caused a momentary consternation at home and abroad; but the new Queen promptly ratified all William's alliances and dispatched Marlborough once more to Holland to rally and enrol the Dutch, and to collect the forces promised by the various allies. Supplies were voted and war was declared on May 4th, 1702.

We may pass over the operations of that year and the next. These were confined for the most part to the recapture of the Dutch fortresses held by the French and were characterized by exasperating obstructions on the part of the Dutch generals and their field deputies, who virtually neutralized the campaign. In September 1703, Archduke Charles was openly proclaimed King of Spain in Vienna, and set out for England under Marlborough's protection on his way to the scene of action in Portugal.

Although the Queen had rewarded him with a dukedom, Marlborough was now so disgusted with the conduct of the allies and the government, that he was on the point of throwing up the command; but the movements of the French at the beginning of the campaign of 1704 opened up a vista so alluring to his energetic mind that the determination was promptly thrown aside, and he embarked on the great move which has established his reputation as one of the foremost military commanders of all time. This was the march from Holland to the Danube, where the army of the Bavarian Elector was gathered as a nucleus for the invasion of Austria. Marlborough's plan involved leaving the Dutch to their own devices, and even persuading them to detach large bodies of their troops, a feat of considerable delicacy which only his consummate tact could have accomplished. The co-operation of Prince Eugene was arranged for, and Marlborough proceeded to convey his entire army across Europe, deceiving the vigilance of the French commanders, and creating a sensation of the first magnitude by his triumphal progress up the Rhine. When he crossed the Neckar, and his destination and objective became apparent, it was too late for a junction to be effected between the French forces under Tallard or Villeroy and the Bavarian army encamped at Ulm. The latter moved to a strong position at Lauingen, and when Marlborough moved northwards with his advance guard of cavalry to skirt the mountainous district, the Elector threw forward a force to hold the pass of the Schellenberg, a fortified place overlooking the town of Donauwörth, at the junction of the river Wörnitz and the Danube in steep and woody country.

During the latter part of his march, Marlborough had encountered his great colleague Eugene, and had been joined by the imperial army under the Margrave Louis of Baden, whom we have already mentioned as the 'Türkensieger' (see p. 39), and whom he had to placate by sharing with him the chief command on alternate days. Camp was formed on the Wörnitz to the north of the Schellenberg, and Marlborough so arranged matters that he was near enough to his objective to attack on the day that he held the command. He had word from Eugene that Villeroy and Tallard were sending reinforcements from Strasbourg, and the natural strength of the position held by the enemy rendered it imperative that there should be no delay. Such was the situation on the eve of the battle of Donauwörth.

1. *Donauwörth*

On the morning of July 2nd, 1704, the picked troops sent forward to lead the attack on the Schellenberg came in sight of the enemy's fortifications, having crossed the Wörnitz on pontoons. Marlborough himself went forward to reconnoitre the position, and seeing that the hill must be approached by a marshy ravine, sent his cavalry into the woods opposite to gather fascines. The designs called *Attacque* and *Fachinade* in the earlier De Hondt series both illustrate this operation. The command of the attack was entrusted to a gallant Dutch general, the first line being led by Brigadier Ferguson, and a forlorn hope of fifty grenadiers going forward under Lord Mordaunt. The Bavarian commanders watching the troops deploying from the wood at first saw no menace, and retired to dine at their ease while their men continued to strengthen the fortifications; even when they found the hills covered with advancing troops they refused to believe that a tired army could attack so late in the day. They were suddenly undeceived by the thunder of guns and the rapid approach of the allied columns. Owing to the thickness of the woods, the attack had to be confined to a single point of the entrenchment where the defence was very strong. The carnage was murderous in the extreme, and the first attack failed, allowing the defenders to sally out and counter-attack with the bayonet. A body of English guards repelled this assault, losing most of their officers, and matters being critical, General Lumley brought his cavalry up as well. A sudden explosion of a magazine threw the enemy into temporary confusion and at the moment when the English and Dutch troops were about to enter the entrenchment, the Margrave's forces arrived on the scene and entered the town of Donauwörth itself, to the right, where the defence had been weakened. During this distraction, Lord John Hay's dragoons were dismounted and thrown into the fray, and finally scattered the enemy. Marlborough, who had exposed himself throughout the battle, led the entrance into the works, and recalling the infantry sent his cavalry in pursuit of the fugitives. Of the entire force of the defenders, a bare 3,000 escaped, leaving the whole of their guns and equipage behind. The allied losses were 1,500 killed and 4,000 wounded, the killed including eight generals and eleven colonels. In a downpour of rain, which made the return journey very difficult, the troops retired to their camp of the night before at Obermorgen.

The Margrave displayed his peculiar character by claiming the entire credit for the victory, and went so far as to have a medal struck in which Marlborough's part in it was ignored. The relations of the two commanders became strained, but outside their circle

Marlborough's pre-eminence was very fully recognized, and although the affair was not one of first-rate importance in itself, he was overwhelmed with flattering acclamations. The Emperor offered him a Bavarian principality and estate, if the Queen would allow him to accept them, and the prestige of his army was greatly increased.

The tapestry (Fig. 40) shows a fair representation of the Schellenberg and the town of Donauwörth beyond it, with three columns of cavalry bringing up fascines, piling them, and retiring at the gallop. In the foreground, on the right, is Marlborough on his white horse, accompanied by two of the staff and one of his running footmen, or field guides, who appear frequently in the tapestries. It is one of the four square panels which decorate the First State Room at Blenheim Palace, and bears at the top the name DUNAWERT with a double-headed eagle and crown in the medallion.

2. Blenheim

On the retirement of the Bavarians to Augsburg, following their defeat at Donauwörth, Marlborough proceeded to lay waste the Elector's country as far as Munich, much against his inclination, for he was a humane commander; but the arrival of a French army under Marshals Tallard and Marsin with thirty thousand troops recalled him to the Danube, where he was joined by the forces under Prince Eugene. The enemy occupied a strongly defended position near the villages of Höchstädt and Blenheim (or Blindheim), where the next engagement, of far greater importance than the first, was destined to take place. Nearly all the races of Europe were represented in the event, each side having an approximately equal force of fifty thousand men. The Margrave of Baden had been detached, to Marlborough's satisfaction, in order to carry out the siege of Ingolstadt, leaving him with the more congenial co-operation of Eugene.

The French combined army, disposed over a wide area, was protected by the stream of the Nebel and marshy ground in front and by the Danube on its right. At the confluence of the two rivers lay the village of Blenheim, behind which was rising ground leading to Oberglau, two miles distant and bounded on the north-west by a range of wooded hills above Lutzingen, where the Elector had his camp. The French had fortified and filled Blenheim with infantry, whose orders were to hold it to the last extremity.

The position having been reconnoitred on the evening of August 12th, 1704, and a plan of battle drawn up, Marlborough, with the piety which was one of his characteristics, spent a portion of the night in prayer and received communion at dawn. The army under Eugene then moved off to the right to engage the Bavarians, the intention being to make a simultaneous attack. Eugene's approach, however, proved to be so difficult that it was midday before Marlborough could move. Lord Cutts was detailed to attack

40. *Donauwörth*, woven by De Vos after L. de Hondt. Blenheim Palace, Duke of Marlborough.

Blenheim and keep the French infantry pinned down, while the main force made its way across the Nebel at a point midway between that village and Oberglau which Marlborough had noted as the weakest spot. The attack on the village failed, General Rowe, who was the first to reach the palisades, falling mortally wounded; but supports continually reinforced the attack and kept the defenders occupied. The main attack also met with extremely severe opposition in its efforts to get across the marshy ground, nor was General Churchill better off opposite the French at Unterglau. So fierce indeed was the attack of the Irish Brigade here that Marlborough foresaw disaster and hurried to his brother's support. Eugene had to rally his cavalry four times before driving back the Bavarians, and when he finally had them behind Lutzingen, both sides were too exhausted to do any more. Eugene himself narrowly escaped being shot by a trooper at short range.

By five o'clock in the afternoon, the battle on the left had progressed so far that Marlborough felt strong enough to make a final cavalry attack in force, under cover of a tremendous cannonade, with the infantry in support across the Nebel. The French broke under the shock, and their right wing was turned and driven headlong towards the Danube, where it was destroyed. Tallard in a vain attempt to restore the centre, ordered the evacuation of Blenheim, but the place was surrounded and he was compelled to surrender at discretion with the flower of his troops. Tallard himself was taken with several generals, and nowhere but in the direction of Lutzingen was there any avenue of retreat. The enemy were reckoned to have lost close upon 40,000 men and officers killed or captured, in comparison with which the losses of the Allies were not severe. The grand army of France, which had been regarded as invincible, received a blow from which it hardly recovered, and for months to come, in the operations which followed, it could not be got to stand. The year ended with the reduction of Landau by siege, and the seizure of Trèves and other places on the Moselle for winter quarters, an arrangement particularly galling for the French, whose own frontier was thereby held under menace until the armies were again in position to take the field. The terror of Marlborough's name in France was such that the very children sang 'Marlbrouck s'en va-t-en guerre'. In England the bitter political rivalry of the time did its utmost to discredit and belittle him, but the populace received him with immense acclaim, and a triumphal procession of the captured booty of Blenheim from the Tower of London to St. James's Park resembled the progress of a Roman conqueror. Parliament voted him a generous reward, and at the Queen's instigation secured to him the royal manor of Woodstock and arranged for the building of Blenheim Palace.

The tapestry (Fig. 42) is a long panel bearing the title HOOGHSTET with a tower, in the centre, and six other arms and names of cities taken in the same campaign (ULM,

41. *A grenadier furling a captured standard*. Detail from the *Battle of Blenheim* (Fig. 42).

INGOLSTAT, PASSAU, VILLINGEN, NORDELINKE, and MEMMINGEN) dispersed in the border, and it shows the attack on the fortified village of Blenheim as the principal feature of the background. The main figures consist as usual of Marlborough (frontispiece) and his staff in brilliant uniforms on the right, and in the centre Marshal Tallard, escorted by two British officers, in the act of surrender. At the left a grenadier is furling one of the captured standards, amid a pile of other booty (Fig. 41). In his dispatch Marlborough specially mentions having taken 'all the tents standing, with their cannon and ammunition, as also a great number of standards, kettle-drums, and colours in the action'. The scene, as usual, is decorative in effect, and suggests rather the modern conception of a Commander-in-Chief's duties outside the struggle than the actual part played by Marlborough, who was strenuously engaged at all points of the affair, and

42. *The Battle of Blenheim*, woven by De Vos after L. de Hondt. Blenheim Palace, Duke of Marlborough.

who led the final charge in person. Indeed his reckless exposure of his own person, however encouraging to the troops, must seem to us imprudent from the point of view of the campaign. In this particular case, the ceremonial grouping is to some extent justified by the incident of the surrender.

3. Forcing the Lines of Brabant

The year 1705 was particularly harassing and exasperating for Marlborough. His carefully laid plan for an invasion of France along the line of the Moselle was frustrated by the non-appearance of his imperial allies under the Margrave of Baden and the failure of supplies. While Marlborough was engaged in a single-handed attempt to besiege Saarlouis, he was recalled to the Netherlands by the supineness of the Dutch, who had allowed Villeroy to capture Huy on the Meuse and Liège. His mere approach, however, was enough to scare the French from Liège, and to drive them behind the fortified lines which they had been constructing for three years between Namur and Antwerp. From the Meuse to Leuwe these lines consisted of a strongly garrisoned breastwork. Beyond, the Gheet river afforded a natural defence. The lines were considered by most authorities impregnable. Marlborough, however, after a close reconnaissance, believed that he could breach them at the junction of the Gheet and Little Gheet, near the village of Elixheim, in the direction of Leuwe. The Dutch generals were as stubborn and impracticable as ever, but having one on whom he could rely, Marlborough detailed him to carry out a feint near Namur, making as though to follow, and having by these means induced Villeroy to leave the upper portion lightly guarded, he made a forced march by night to the point intended, leaving the Dutch to follow as soon as their work was ended. Everything possible was done to disguise the object of the march, the troopers carrying bundles of hay instead of fascines.

On the morning of July 18th, 1705, under cover of a dense mist, the army arrived at its objective and attacked the defences in three columns which quickly secured the villages of Neer Wenden and Neer Hespen, the bridge and village of Elixheim, and a castle called Wange which commanded the passage of the Little Gheet. The impetuosity of the attack was such that the troops did not wait for bridges to be thrown over, but breached and passed the fortifications almost without obstacle. Not until the troops were across them and were ready to form did a strong cavalry force appear under the Marquis d'Allegre, which Marlborough charged in person. The affair was hotly contested for about an hour, during which Marlborough himself was cut off with a single orderly and narrowly escaped being killed. The French, however, were finally routed and driven off, and when Villeroy arrived on the scene there was nothing for him to do but to retreat with so much precipitation that his army did not stop until it had crossed the

43. *Forcing the Lines of Brabant*, woven by De Vos after L. de Hondt. Blenheim Palace, Duke of Marlborough.

Dyle and taken refuge under the guns of Louvain.* Marlborough followed him, and if he could have forced an engagement would probably have succeeded in inflicting another Blenheim; but the timidity and even malevolence of the Dutch commanders prevented the attack, and the campaign for that year was left inconclusive. The lines, however, were destroyed and Brabant opened up, and Marlborough spent the rest of the season in composing difficulties and settling negotiations in Vienna and Berlin. As usual his enemies at home threw all the blame for failure on his shoulders, although the Dutch under pressure were compelled to withdraw the worst of their generals from future activity, and to that extent lightened his troubles.

The tapestry (Fig. 43) depicting the breach of the *Lines of Brabant* corresponds very accurately with the topographical plan. One can see the winding line of the fortifications with the village and bridge of Elixheim and, right in the centre, the castle of Wange. In the background is the cavalry engagement and in the distance on the left the hills of Tirlemont with the main road along which the retreat took place. Marlborough, however, instead of being in the actual conflict, is shown issuing directions from a high point in the foreground, for purposes of decorative effect. There being no town arms available, the border contains the Churchill arms instead, and for many years the incident has been wrongly associated with the siege of Lille.

Ramillies

It is a remarkable fact, for which there is no complete explanation, that the Battle of Ramillies, perhaps the most brilliant of Marlborough's successes, is not represented among the Blenheim tapestries (see App. I), although no fewer than three hangings are devoted to the siege of Bouchain in 1711.

The campaign to which this battle belongs was in the nature of an afterthought, Marlborough's intention having been to leave the obstructive Dutch to their own devices, after his experience of the previous year, and to join Prince Eugene in carrying on the war in Italy. The Austrians desired him to continue the promising manœuvres on the Moselle, but his knowledge of the assistance he might count on from the Margrave of Baden disinclined him to embark upon these again. Moreover, the French themselves suddenly attacked the Margrave and inflicted a series of reverses on him in the neighbourhood of the upper Rhine, which so alarmed the Dutch that they hastily threw

* The panegyric on Marlborough's column in Blenheim Park refers to Brabant thus: 'The French . . . retired behind Intrenchments which they deemed impregnable. The Duke forced these In- trenchments, with inconsiderable loss, on the seventh day of July one thousand seven hundred and five. He defeated a great part of the Army which defended them. The Rest escaped by a precipitate Retreat.'

themselves on the protection of Marlborough, and promised him any reasonable concessions if he would not desert them. In these circumstances Marlborough decided to abandon the Italian campaign and prepared instead to besiege Namur.

This project brought Villeroy, the French Marshal, with the Bavarian Elector, hotfoot to the Netherlands, and although they tried to avoid a decisive meeting, Marlborough by quick marches succeeded in bringing them to bay on the Mont St. André, a strong position overlooking the village of Ramillies. In the battle which followed the French were swiftly and completely routed with the loss of 15,000 men, their baggage and most of their guns. Louvain, Brussels, and Ghent were set free, and shortly afterwards Ostend was besieged and taken. This meant that practically all Flanders was now wrested from the French.

These were the great results of the campaign of 1706. The Dutch, however, interposed as usual to prevent the reduction of Mons. The following year was barren of any outstanding event, and is chiefly noteworthy for the political intrigues which threatened to undermine Marlborough's position at home while he was engaged in composing the quarrels of all the allies abroad.

4. Oudenarde

When the armies reassembled for the campaign of 1708 the French took the initiative by planning an attack on the strong fortress of Oudenarde, a key position to the Dutch defences, the capture of which would have undone all the work of the previous years. Issuing from Braine L'Alleud, and hoping to throw Marlborough off his guard, they successfully occupied Ghent and Bruges, but before they could reach Oudenarde, the pursuit was in full cry, and both armies reached the Scheldt at about the same time on July 11th, 1708. Marlborough had detached an advance guard under General Cadogan, his admirable Quartermaster-General, to occupy a position at Lessines and bridge the river, and at the same time he had managed to throw a garrison into the town before it was invested. His own approach with the cavalry was made at the gallop, so urgent was the call. On the eve of the engagement he was joined, to his great pleasure, by Prince Eugene, with whom he divided the command. Another prince who fought under him that day was the Elector of Hanover, the future George II.

The battle which followed the crossing of the Scheldt and the relief of the fortress was hotly contested, and, in view of the wide expanse of country covered and the isolated nature of the many operations, is exceedingly complicated to follow. It was by no means a foregone conclusion and might have ended quite differently but for the dissensions which broke out between the two French commanders, Vendôme and the Duke of Burgundy, who cancelled each other's orders and paralysed the defence.

44. *Village and troops.* Detail from *Oudenarde* (Fig. 45).

As it was, the battle lasted all day, and it was not until the dusk of evening that the last stand of the French was broken and their army finally driven off in rout.

The tapestry (Fig. 45), labelled ALDENARDA below the medallion with the town arms, as usual shows Marlborough and his staff in the foreground, apparently paying scant attention to the operations in the distance. One may hazard a conjecture that the officer with his back turned, on the extreme left, is the Elector of Hanover, and the one holding out his hat Prince Eugene in the act of galloping off to take up his independent command.* On the side opposite to the group is a mythological river god typifying the Scheldt and holding out a plan of the fortress.

Immediately below in the middle distance are the bridges over the river and the troops crossing in column formation. On the far side they are advancing to their various

* Marlborough's detractors at home did not fail to try and raise jealousy between the two commanders as to their respective parts in the victory, to which Marlborough's dignified answer was: 'I dare say Prince Eugene and I shall never differ about our share of laurels.'

45. *Oudenarde*, woven by De Vos after L. de Hondt. Blenheim Palace, Duke of Marlborough.

positions in the battle, and the topography with its many villages, mills, etc., is extremely detailed and accurate (Fig. 44).

5, 6. *Wynendael* and *The Surrender of Lille*

Immediately after the battle of Oudenarde, Marlborough moved his army across to Menin, having detached a force to seize the lines which the French had constructed from Ypres to Warneton in order to protect the country lying between the Scheldt and the Lys. He had word that Marshal Boufflers was in Lille, and he decided to lay siege to it as a preliminary move in the invasion of France. The city had been captured by Louis XIV in 1667, and fortified with elaborate outworks and a citadel of pentagon-form by Vauban after its cession in the treaty of Aix-la-Chapelle. It was garrisoned by 15,000 men, consisting largely of the fugitives from Oudenarde.

It was arranged that Eugene should take command of the siege when he could bring his army and supplies up from Brussels, and that Marlborough should command the covering army. These operations took a month to complete, during which the Duke remained inactive, while at home his Duchess was vigorously fomenting a breach with the Queen. Finally the siege was opened on August 13th, 1708, and began to drag out its weary length while Marlborough held in check the attempts of Vendôme and the Duke of Berwick to relieve the city. His impatience found frequent expression in dispatches home, but the besiegers were hampered by shortage of supplies and ammunition. On September 20th, Eugene was wounded by a round shot, and the Duke took over his command. The arrival of a naval force at Ostend gave him the opportunity of ordering up a large convoy, round which for several days the attention of both sides was concentrated, the French being determined to intercept it. The convoy started on September 27th, and Marlborough sent forward a force of twelve battalions under General Webb to reinforce the escort, as well as a body of horse under General Cadogan. The latter came on the French in the neighbourhood of Wynendael, and went back to report. Webb took his infantry forward, and having posted them in a pair of coppices on either side of a narrow gap, advanced beyond it with a small body of men in order to draw the enemy into his ambush just as the convoy was approaching the spot. The plan was completely successful, and the grenadiers posted in the woods opened a destructive fire on the massed columns of the French, first from one side and then from the other. As they were retiring in some disorder, the cavalry under Cadogan arrived on the scene and proposed to charge the retreat, but this was not considered advisable as the convoy was now secure and able to complete its journey.

The action took place on September 28th, and was a brilliant little affair marred unfortunately by an error in the dispatches, which gave all the credit to Cadogan and

46. *Wynendael*, woven by De Vos after L. de Hondt. Blenheim Palace, Duke of Marlborough.

passed over the superior claims of Webb. The scene at mess when the gazette arrived from England has been graphically described in Thackeray's *Henry Esmond*; but Marlborough, whom Webb blamed, seems to have been genuinely vexed at the occurrence, and took considerable pains to put Webb right with the authorities at home, urging that he should be given immediate promotion.* Webb, however, retired from the campaign for a time, and in spite of very flattering compliments in the House of Commons, nursed his grievance volubly and gave active support to the attacks on Marlborough, which were beginning to undermine his position.

Meanwhile the siege went on more actively, despite the opening of the sluices by Vendôme, which flooded the country and added to the besiegers' difficulties. On October 22nd, Boufflers was constrained to call a parley, and the city was surrendered on the following day. The citadel held out until December, when the area was effectively occupied and garrisoned by the Allies.

The tapestry labelled WYNENDAEL (Fig. 46) is one of the smaller pieces, and depicts a portion of the convoy escorted by musketeers and pikemen.† In the background are the English forces drawn up in three long lines across the gap, with the French in retreat beyond. The two coppices are clearly indicated.

The panel entitled INSULAE (Fig. 47), with a fleur-de-lis in the medallion, represents the surrender of Marshal Boufflers to Marlborough, who has dismounted and is addressing one of his staff. In the background can be seen the city of Lille (L'Isle) and its approaches, with clouds of smoke rising from the conflagrations. The representation of Boufflers bears considerable resemblance to his engraved portraits and is one of the few instances in which definite identification is possible.

7. *Malplaquet*

In 1709 Villars replaced Vendôme in the command of the French army of the Netherlands. The Allies laid siege to Tournai, which fell at the end of August, and proceeded thence to the investment of Mons in Hainault. The Prince of Hesse was sent forward to seize upon strategic positions in the neighbourhood, while the French advanced in their full strength to the relief. On September 7th Boufflers joined Villars and the two armies encountered each other in the wide plain watered by the Haine and the Trouille and

* The panegyric on Marlborough's column in Blenheim Park says in reference to Wynendael: '. . . the necessary convoys arrived in safety. One alone was attacked. The troops which attacked it, were beat.'

† It is curious to reflect that pikemen still formed part of the regular forces. The manuals of pike-drill were in force up to the opening of the eighteenth century. The firelock musket with flint and steel did not begin to replace the matchlock before 1677.

47. *The Surrender of Lille*, woven by De Vos after L. de Hondt. Blenheim Palace, Duke of Marlborough.

bounded on the south by the woods of Lagnière and Jansart. With their wings resting on these woods the French threw up a series of strong fortifications. Marlborough had to wait for the arrival of Prince Eugene, and it was not until the morning of the 11th that he felt himself strong enough, under cover of a dense mist, to move his forces into position for an engagement. The French, in addition to their defences, were for once in superior strength. Marlborough's plan was to attack the centre under cover of a feint by the Dutch against the French right, but the misplaced eagerness of the Prince of Orange turned this into a serious assault and involved his forces in a terrible slaughter which delayed the main operation. After four hours' fighting, the breastwork and part of the wood on the French left was carried, and Marshal Villars had been so badly wounded that he had to leave the field. Boufflers, however, continued the resistance with great gallantry, and at a critical moment, when the centre redan had been taken and guns mounted on it to rake the cavalry behind, he rallied the French *gendarmerie* in a series of magnificent charges, which Marlborough's cavalry with difficulty withstood. Finally, finding his centre pierced, his right dislodged and his left cut off from support, Boufflers was forced to retire in the direction of Bavai, leaving the Allies in possession of the field. The Allies had lost some 5,500 killed and 12,700 wounded or missing, the heaviest casualties they had ever suffered, while the French probably lost about 14,000 all told, but were able to carry out their retirement in good order. Among their general officers who earned special distinction was a D'Artagnan, who had three horses killed under him, and was rewarded with the rank of Marshal. Mons capitulated in the following month.

The losses at Malplaquet were a cause of much discontent, both at home and in the army, Marlborough himself being blamed for them, somewhat unfairly as his force was 10,000 men short of the number he had asked for. The French, on the other hand, regarded it as the most serious of their reverses.

The tapestry (Fig. 48) bears the title MONTES HANNONIAE (Mons in Hainault)—a name taken from the siege and not from the plain of which the village of Malplaquet was a key position. The arms in the medallion are a castle. In the foreground of the subject, Marlborough with two mounted officers on the left is dispatching an aide-de-camp with orders. An officer, possibly Colonel Armstrong, mounted on a white horse is riding up the hill towards the Duke. Immediately below, on the right, the British battalions are attacking the Sart Wood, from which they drove the French after two hours of hand to hand fighting; a battery on the left is supporting them in flank. Across the centre can be seen the French breastworks, with four long lines of troops behind them, and other batteries in action. Lord Orkney with fifteen or twenty battalions is advancing to the main attack, while the Dutch are engaged on the left. The scene is the open plain, with

48. *Malplaquet*, woven by De Vos after L. de Hondt. Blenheim Palace, Duke of Marlborough.

the village which gave its name to the battle on the right, and rising ground in the far distance.

8, 9, 10. *The Siege of Bouchain*

At the opening of the campaign of 1711, and what proved to be the conclusion of nine years of war, we find the French army under Marshal Villars firmly posted behind a long fortified line of the sort in which it specialized so highly. These defences, designed to keep the Allies from invading France itself, stretched from the coast near Calais to Namur, following the course of the Sensée and the Scarpe to Arras, and were well protected by a series of fortresses, which included Douai, Cambrai, Valenciennes, and Bouchain, near the confluence of the Sensée and the Scheldt. As usual the lines were regarded as impregnable,* and Marlborough, having formed the intention of seizing one of the fortresses and opening up the road to France, was forced to adopt a policy of absolute secrecy which extended to his own staff. The strategy by which he disguised his plans was of the highest possible order. The death of the Emperor Joseph and trouble on the Rhine had deprived him temporarily of the assistance of Prince Eugene, and he was in no condition to risk a pitched battle on ground so strongly prepared; yet all his movements were carefully contrived to give the opposite impression, and having by a most ingenious ruse drawn the defences of the little village of Arleux, which menaced his objective, and collected the main forces of Villars in the place where he wanted them, he executed a forced march of thirty-six miles, under cover of darkness, with his entire army, seized and bridged the passage of the Sensée, and was across the lines before he could be intercepted or attacked. The way being then open, he proceeded to invest and capture Bouchain.

Bouchain consisted of a main fortress at the junction of the Sensée and the Scheldt, protected by both and by a wide extent of marshland, together with a strong entrenchment, a hornwork, and a series of redoubts. Every possible means was employed to hinder and distract the advance, but without effect. The British troops made their way through the marshy ground, wading up to their necks and carrying their arms over their heads. Having gained the required positions they proceeded to build a circumvallation round the fortress, and within a few weeks had so reduced the garrison by gunfire that it was forced to surrender at discretion.

Marlborough justly considered the capture of Bouchain one of his greatest achievements,† and if fortune, at the hands of his political enemies, had not deserted him, and

* Villars, in a famous dispatch to the King, alluded to them boastfully as the 'ne plus ultra'.

† Bishop Burnet reflects the impression which this brilliant forcing of the French lines made among right-minded people in England. (Gilbert Burnet, *History of His Own Time*, ed. 1823, passim.)

49. *Bouchain II*, woven by De Vos after L. de Hondt. Blenheim Palace, Duke of Marlborough.

50. *Bouchain I*, woven by De Vos after L. de Hondt. Blenheim Palace, Duke of Marlborough.

51. *Bouchain III*, woven by De Vos after L. de Hondt. Blenheim Palace, Duke of Marlborough.

peace put an end to the campaign, there is no saying how much further he might have carried his successes against the French.

As it is, the operations are shown in no fewer than three tapestries, with minute exactness, the view in all cases being from the east looking towards the west.

In the first tapestry (Fig. 50), a long panel, we are shown the staff with Marlborough in the centre galloping across the foreground from the right. In the background is the general advance in four long columns towards the town, which is clearly seen beyond the tree on the left. So accurate and clear is the tapestry that the movements of the troops and the topography shown in it correspond closely to the plans and descriptions given by Archdeacon Coxe.

The second (Fig. 49) is one of the smaller panels and shows the first stages of the work of circumvallation. The fortress, with the French and Swiss defenders drawn up within it, can be clearly seen, but the hornwork is hidden by the two large mounted figures on the right. On the left is the Scheldt, with an empty redoubt which the allies have either captured or surprised before it could be occupied, and the passage of the river is in progress. In the distance is the Sensée, which protected the fortifications on the west by a plainly visible loop.

In the third panel (Fig. 51) we see the circumvallation completed, with the parallels and other details of the siege. To the left is the French encampment. The Duke, with his staff, is posted as usual under a large tree, accompanied by two of the running footmen. A body of officers in the near distance is riding towards the group, perhaps to announce the surrender, and on the right a staff officer is galloping away with dispatches, followed by a large hound which, tradition says, belonged to Cadogan and was accustomed to follow him in the field (Fig. 52). It seems questionable, however, whether a general of Cadogan's rank would be employed on the service in question.

Immediately under the tree, with his right arm crooked, is an officer in a blue coat on a white horse who may represent Colonel Armstrong, Marlborough's chief engineer. There is a portrait at Blenheim in which the features are not dissimilar. In both the other Bouchain tapestries an officer in a blue coat accompanies the commander and may be intended for the same person. Apart from this conjecture, individual members of the staff, owing to the full-bottomed wigs, are extremely difficult to identify.

Bouchain was Marlborough's last victory. Recalled to England in disgrace, owing to the triumph of his enemies and the quarrel of his Duchess with the Queen, he found himself faced by heavy financial charges and a general accusation of self-aggrandizement and avarice which were difficult to meet. The death of his one friend Godolphin in September 1712 left him isolated, and he quitted the country in October. The Duchess

52. *Staff officer and hound*. Detail from *Bouchain III* (Fig. 51).

joined him at Aix-la-Chapelle, and they moved to Frankfurt, visiting the estate of Mindelheim, which had been conferred on him after Blenheim. This he shortly afterwards lost on its restoration to Bavaria. For some time he was at Hanover, working for the Protestant succession, and on August 1st, 1714, he returned to England on the news of the Queen's fatal illness. From that time he took little part in public affairs. His strength was much shaken by the strenuous nature of his life, and on June 22nd, 1722, he died. He was buried in Westminster Abbey, his body being removed later to a mausoleum in the chapel at Blenheim, the private memorial of his many victories, for public monument had he none.

Time has vindicated the great Duke of Marlborough and acquitted him of the petty charges brought by an ungrateful country, which he had saved. One of his panegyrists, Sir John Fortescue, described him as 'the greatest man and the greatest soldier that has ever stood at the head of a British army',[2] and speculates on what the extent of his successes would have been had he ever been in real command, unhampered by the machinations of enemies at home and the obstructions of the Allies in the field, with whom he was compelled to work and whom he was obliged to humour.

CHAPTER VII

OTHER CONTEMPORARY TAPESTRIES

The 'Art of War': Second Version (a)

IN Chapters IV and V we dealt with tapestries based on the First Version of the *Art of War* by Lambert de Hondt, and in Chapter VI we examined the Blenheim 'Victories'. We now come to a third series, which combines aspects of the previous two, with details often reused or reversed from the first series, and with excerpts from the 'Victories', and is based on a second version of the *Art of War*. The numerous sets in this series were commissioned by princes and generals who had fought either with or against the Grand Alliance to commemorate their share in the campaigns. In the case of those who fought against it, however, this share could hardly have given much cause for gratification.

The first of these antagonists, and the most important, was the same Elector Maximilian Emmanuel, who had commissioned the original De Hondt series. Having thrown in his lot with Louis XIV and taken a prominent part in the battle of Blenheim, where he was so heavily defeated, Maximilian Emmanuel was driven from Bavaria and deprived of his dominions in 1704, and spent the remainder of the war as a commander in the French army of the Netherlands. He co-operated with Marshal Villeroy in the operations of 1705, which led to the occupation of Huy and Liège. He was again defeated by Marlborough when the lines of Brabant were forced that same year, and was in joint command with Villeroy at Ramillies, where they were so disastrously defeated.

After the conclusions of hostilities in 1711, Maximilian Emmanuel was restored to his dominions by the Treaty of Baden (1714) and busied himself in the completion of a new palace at Schleissheim, not far from Munich, which he re-entered in 1715. For this he commissioned a large set of military tapestries. Possessing already the original series, and not wishing to duplicate them exactly, he seems to have ordered from De Hondt's studio a fresh set of similar subjects in which the details were redesigned and the composition, as a rule, reversed.

The Schleissheim Set (c. 1724)

The Schleissheim tapestries as a whole consist of no fewer than fourteen pieces (Nos. 1–14). The new subjects are differentiated where pertinent from the original ones by

53. C. Vermeulen after J. Vivien: *Maximilian Emmanuel of Bavaria*. Engraving.

the figure ii. All but one (No. 7) of Nos. 1–8 are to be found at Schleissheim (the first six listed here in the same order as the Munich Set).

1. *Campement ii* (Fig. 54).

2. *Fachinade ii* (Fig. 55), which is here a narrow panel without side borders. As the complete subject is not shown this tapestry seems to be an entrefenêtre. *Attacque* is not repeated but is combined with *Fachinade*.

3. *Embuscade ii* (Fig. 56).

4. *Pillage ii* (Fig. 57).

5. *La Marche ii* (Fig. 58), a design which lends itself so aptly to portraiture that it

91

54. *Campement ii*, woven by De Vos after L. de Hondt. Schleissheim Set. Schleissheim, New Palace.

may well have attracted the special attention of Maximilian Emmanuel, and we shall see that it was generally popular for the same reason.

6. *Fouragement ii* (Fig. 59).

7. *La Halte* (Fig. 60), a new composition to which we venture to give a new name, represents an army resting on the march. The tapestry is shown here surrounded by a border pieced together from fragments belonging to the earlier series. Three of the titled anvils (those for *Campement*, *Embuscade*, and *Pillage*) are inappropriately included in the border (cf. pp. 32, 34). This panel formerly hung in the Munich Residenz but is now missing from Schleissheim. It is the property of the Wittelsbacher Ausgleichsfonds, as are also the *Fachinade* and the *Attacque* of the Munich Set (see p. 36), but is apparently not at present on view.

8. *Sea Fight* (Fig. 61) is a curious subject for the Elector, who possessed no navy and was not concerned with any naval engagement. It has been described variously as the *Battle of La Hogue* and the *Sinking of the Spanish Silver Fleet at Vigo*. If any definite

55. *Fachinade ii*,
woven by De Vos after L. de Hondt.
Schleissheim Set. Schleissheim, New Palace.

56. *Embuscade ii*, woven by De Vos after L. de Hondt. Schleissheim Set. Schleissheim, New Palace.

57. *Pillage ii*, woven by De Vos after L. de Hondt. Schleissheim Set. Schleissheim, New Palace.

58. *La Marche ii*, woven by De Vos after L. de Hondt. Schleissheim Set. Schleissheim, New Palace.

59. *Fouragement ii*, woven by De Vos after L. de Hondt. Schleissheim Set. Schleissheim, New Palace.

60. *La Halte*, woven by De Vos after L. de Hondt. Schleissheim Set. Munich, Wittelsbacher Ausgleichsfonds.

61. *Sea Fight*, woven by De Vos after L. de Hondt. Schleissheim Set. Schleissheim, New Palace.

incident is intended, the former is the more probable of the two, although it did not take place in the War of the Spanish Succession but in 1692.

In some cases duplicates are to be found in Munich at the National Museum. Among the latter are *La Marche* and *Sea Fight*, both without borders.

To the next six panels we give the titles they bear in the palace inventory.

9. *Maximilian Emmanuel and his Staff—three figures* (Fig. 62).

10. *Maximilian Emmanuel and his Staff at a Siege* (Fig. 63).

11. *Maximilian Emmanuel and his Staff—six figures* (Fig. 64).

12. *Maximilian Emmanuel and two Officers (on foot)* (Fig. 65).

13. *Wagon with Foot Soldiers* (Fig. 66).

14. *A small body of Cavalry crossing a Plain* (Fig. 67).

The last of these was woven at the Munich tapestry works in 1724.[1] It hangs with its right border covered by the overlapping left border of No. 10 (cf. Fig. 63).

The following two additional panels (Nos. 15 and 16), included here for convenience of reference, which have long been hung with this set and are to be found in the inventory, belong to the 1696 Le Clerc and Van der Borcht version and have been described with the Munich Set (see pp. 36–8).

15. *A mounted trooper questioning a peasant* (Fig. 17).

16. *A forager whipping up his horse* (Fig. 18).

The last three (Nos. 14, 15, and 16) are used as entrefenêtres, added to fill up space.

The five panels Nos. 9–13 are truly remarkable, considering the situation in which they are found. It may be mentioned that the new series was woven by De Vos, not by the former craftsmen, and these five panels are taken straight from the cartoons from which De Vos wove specially for the Duke of Marlborough. They are indeed portions from the Blenheim 'Victories'.

No. 9 (Fig. 62) is the principal group from the the *Lines of Brabant* (Fig. 43). In this panel, however, the head of a second officer, missing from the Blenheim Palace tapestry, can be seen behind the Commander-in-Chief.

No. 10 (Fig. 63) is a free variant of the third *Bouchain* panel (Fig. 51), with Cadogan's hound omitted.

No. 11 (Fig. 64) is actually a group from the *Hooghstet* (or *Blenheim*) panel (Fig. 42).

No. 12 (Fig. 65) is the standing group of Marlborough and his officers from *Insulae* (or the *Surrender of Lille*) (Fig. 47) with the figure of Marshal Boufflers surrendering the fortress omitted.

No. 13 (Fig. 66) is a portion of the Blenheim *Wynendael* (Fig. 46).

62. *Maximilian Emmanuel and his Staff—three figures,*
woven by De Vos after L. de Hondt.
Schleissheim Set. Schleissheim, New Palace.

63. *Maximilian Emmanuel and his Staff at a Siege*, woven by De Vos after L. de Hondt. Schleissheim Set. Schleissheim, New Palace.

In these cases the portraiture, no doubt, has been amended to suit the features of the Elector (Fig. 53), noticeably in Nos. 9 and 10 (Figs. 62, 63), though the uniforms and the other figures appear to be little changed. In only one case (No. 10) has an attempt been made to furnish the scene with details suggesting an actual operation in which the Elector has been engaged, such as the Siege of Huy. The background of this panel depicts some definite incident in a siege which the Bavarian Kriegsarchiv was unfortunately unable to identify. Apart from this, the subjects are devoid of any distinctive features which illustrate the Elector's doings at any stage of the campaign; and we can

64. *Maximilian Emmanuel and his Staff—six figures*,
woven by De Vos after L. de Hondt.
Schleissheim Set. Schleissheim, New Palace.

65. *Maximilian Emmanuel and two Officers (on foot)*,
woven by De Vos after L. de Hondt.
Schleissheim Set. Schleissheim, New Palace.

66. *Wagon with Foot Soldiers*,
    woven by De Vos after L. de Hondt.
    Schleissheim Set. Schleissheim, New Palace.

67. *A small body of Cavalry crossing a Plain*,
    woven at Munich in 1724.
    Schleissheim Set. Schleissheim, New Palace.

only wonder at the grim humour or perhaps cynical indifference of De Vos, the Flemish weaver, which has led to this substitution of the Elector's portrait for that of his victorious adversary in a series of scenes representing the latter's achievements. That the Battle of Blenheim, which cost the Elector his dominions, should fall into this category, seems almost past belief. Technically it may be said that there was nothing unusual or immoral in the transaction, since from time immemorial cartoons have remained the property of the weaver and have been used over and over again, as in the case of the famous Raphael designs for the *Acts of the Apostles*.

Several panels from the Schleissheim Set bear the signature of De Vos. Their trophy borders, which have a general resemblance to those of the Munich Set of 1696, embody certain details also from those of the first Blenheim Palace set (cf., e.g., Figs. 26, 54). They must therefore have been woven later than the Blenheim panels. Schleissheim, begun in 1701, was not completed until about 1722,* and the date on the Munich-woven entrefenêtre (Fig. 67) indicates that the tapestries were delivered or completed some two years later.†

The Archbishop Clemens August Set

Dr. Göbel very kindly called our attention to the following passage in an inventory (now in the archives at Düsseldorf)² made of the contents of the Residenz in Bonn, on the death of the Archbishop Clemens August in 1761:

> *In der Zweyten antichambre Nr. 1. Drey stück von hautelisse den feldzügen des churfürsten Maximilian aus Bayern Höchst seel[n] Andenken In Flanderen Vorstellend.*
>
> *Im Audienz Saal.*
> *Nr. 1. Vier stück tapeten von hautelisse von vorig-gemeltem flandrischen feldzug.*
> *N.B. das achte Stück zu dieser tenture gehörig, befindet sich auf die garde meuble.*
> *Nr. 13. Einige stück von denen gnädigst angeschafften bordures zu denen obgemelten tapeten gehörig, so noch nicht alle vollständig fertig.*

Archbishop Clemens August, Elector of Cologne, was a younger son of the Elector Maximilian Emmanuel and it is therefore not surprising that he had a set of tapestries supposed to represent his father's campaigns in Flanders. As he did not become Arch-

---

* Though begun in 1701, the work on the Palace at Schleissheim remained in abeyance from 1704 to 1714, when fresh plans were designed for it by the architect De Cotte, who was succeeded by Effner in 1719. Maximilian Emmanuel himself did not return to Bavaria until April 10th, 1715 (see p. 90). The wall-paintings in the Victoriasaal deal with the old events of the Turkish war of 1683 and onwards, and have no reference to the recent campaigns. The Elector probably preferred to dwell on the memory of his earlier successes.

† The *Conquest of Tunis* tapestries, though ordered in 1712, were not delivered by De Vos until 1721 (see p. 14).

bishop of Cologne until 1723 the tapestries in his possession are most likely to have been related to the Schleissheim Set, which as we have seen were delivered to the Elector Maximilian Emmanuel about that time. Further, the Schleissheim Set, having been made after the War of the Spanish Succession, was presumably intended to refer to Maximilian Emmanuel's campaigns in Flanders, whereas the Munich Set of 1696 celebrated his Turkish Wars. Therefore, if a conjecture may be permitted, we would suggest that the set of eight tapestries owned by Archbishop Clemens August was a replica of the Schleissheim Set, which contained eight panels and was made for his father. There is probably now no hope of tracing these tapestries, because Archbishop Clemens August's collections after his death in 1761 were sold by auction in 1762, 1764, and 1768, and any of the remaining furniture and other effects once belonging to him were probably destroyed in the fire at the Residenz in Bonn in 1777.[3] In any case, if the tapestries of Archbishop Clemens August were sold by auction, some of the various borderless replicas here listed of individual panels of the Schleissheim version may well have come from his collection.

The 'Art of War': Second Version (b)

Other sets

Fragmentary sets and isolated specimens of the second De Hondt *Art of War* are by no means uncommon, both in England and on the Continent. Except in a very few cases they have been removed from their original abodes and dispersed by sale. The following list gives particulars of all those which the author has been able to trace.

I. At the royal palace in Dresden, before the First World War, there was a set of five, acquired by Augustus the Strong, King of Saxony, with whom Marlborough had some dealings. Saxon troops, in fact, fought at Malplaquet, but not at Blenheim. These tapestries were sold in 1926 to the firm of Margraf, in Berlin.[4]

The most important of them is a version of the Blenheim Palace *Hooghstet* or *Höchstädt* (Fig. 69), with a considerable alteration on the left side. Instead of the grenadier displaying the captured flags and trophies, there is a large fortified building with a moat or weir in front, and although the battle details are omitted the panel seems to have gone by its proper name.[5] This panel was sold at Sotheby's in 1964.[6]

The remaining four subjects all belong to the Second Version of the *Art of War* (cf. the Schleissheim Set, Figs. 54–61) and consist of: *Campement ii*, *Fachinade ii*, *La Marche ii*, and *La Halte*. The borders correspond to those at Schleissheim, and two of the panels bear the signature of J. de Vos.*

* Either *La Marche ii* or *La Halte* may be the panel said to have been owned by Hitler.

68. *Pillage ii*, woven by De Vos after L. de Hondt. Pourtalès Set. Formerly Drakelowe, Sir Robert Gresley, Bt.

69. *The Battle of Blenheim*, woven by De Vos after L. de Hondt. Saxon Set. Formerly Dresden, Royal Palace.

II. At Schloss Ivenack, in Mecklenburg, belonging to Graf von Plessen, there were four panels without borders: *Campement ii*, *La Marche ii*, *La Halte*, and *Sea Fight*. It is probable that a Von Plessen was engaged in the operations, on one side or the other, although his name does not appear in the histories.

III. At Schloss Neudeck, Upper Silesia, belonging to Prince von Donnersmarck, there was a single tapestry of *La Marche ii* with the Schleissheim border.

IV. At the Banque de Belgique, Brussels, now defunct, there existed formerly five panels, without borders, which were lent to the Brussels Exhibition of 1880.[7] The subjects were: *Campement ii*, *Pillage ii*, *Fouragement ii* (two fragments only), and *Sea Fight*. Where these tapestries are now is unknown.

V. At Drakelowe, near Burton-on-Trent, the residence of the late Sir Robert Gresley, Bt., there were three fine panels, unfortunately without borders, representing: *Fachinade ii* (Fig. 70), *Pillage ii* (Fig. 68), and *La Halte*. The first is the complete panel of which the example at Schleissheim is only a portion. The set had formerly belonged to the Pourtalès family, and an ancestor of that family may well have taken part in the war. The tapestries were sold as five pieces at Christie's on April 3rd, 1924, but were later reunited. As not infrequently happens with these subjects, they were catalogued as belonging to the Flanders campaign of Louis XIV, after Van der Meulen, and attributed to the Gobelins factory. Actually they were, of course, woven by De Vos at Brussels like all the others, although they bear no signature. The *La Halte* and *Fachinade* panels were later sold for Lady Frances Gresley, after her husband's death, at Sotheby's on May 28th, 1937, to Mrs. B. Brocklebank, Gifford's Hall, Stoke-by-Nayland, Suffolk.

VI. At Calehill Park, Ashford, Kent, the residence of the late Sir Chester Beatty, there was a panel of *La Marche ii*, surrounded by an eighteenth-century picture-frame border. It once belonged to the Munich firm of Bernheimer[8] and thence passed to a private owner in Sweden, who lent it for some time to the National Museum in Stockholm[9] and finally sold it to Chester Beatty (cf. No. VIII below). The tapestry was sold in the 1950s through Frank Partridge and Sons Ltd., to a private collector, address unknown.

VII. Sir Philip Sassoon owned two panels, *Campement ii* and *La Marche ii*, the latter signed J. De Vos. They have trophy borders above and below corresponding to the ones at Schleissheim, except for a special banner with an armorial device on the left of the central enrichment at the top. They do not represent the subjects completely, and since they have never had any side borders, must have been intended as entrefenêtres. The pair formerly belonged to the late Lord Brassey, and were acquired from his sale at Christie's on May 19th, 1920.

70. *Fachinade ii*, woven by De Vos after L. de Hondt. Pourtalès Set. Formerly Drakelowe, Sir Robert Gresley, Bt.

VIII. At The Fine Arts Gallery of San Diego, California, to which it was presented by Mr. and Mrs. Appleton S. Bridges, there is a version of the *Pillage ii* panel, in a picture-frame border with distinctive enrichments. It formed one of a pair sold at the Galerie Georges Petit in Paris on June 7th, 1905, the companion piece (with an identical border) being *La Halte*, the present ownership of which is unknown.

The New York *Art News*, in which the San Diego piece was illustrated,[10] describes it as 'The Plunder of Pfalz, a seventeenth-century Gobelins tapestry from a cartoon by Anton Frans van der Meulen[11] (b. Brussels 1634, d. Paris 1690)', and adds 'it is one of a series of six, four of the others representing war-scenes, the other, now in the National Gallery at Stockholm, representing Louis XIV himself on horseback surrounded by men of his military Service'. All that need be said about this farrago of misinformation is that the last-mentioned panel is the one just catalogued (No. VI above) as formerly belonging to Chester Beatty.

IX. There is at the Petit Palais in Paris, belonging to the Collection Dutuit, an entrefenêtre showing part of *Campement ii*, with the man blowing a trumpet and a rider about to mount. It has in the top and bottom borders the characteristic trophy ornament and pile of camp equipment associated with the Schleissheim Set. As in so many other cases, it is wrongly labelled a Gobelins tapestry after Van der Meulen.

X. Yet another replica of *Campement ii* was sold at Christie's on June 12th, 1929 (Lot 119), and was bought by M. Founès of Paris (cf. p. 41). It had no border and was said to have come from an Austrian collection.

XI. Another example of *La Marche ii* is in the cathedral at Vilna and has been published by Morelowski.[12] It may have been given to the cathedral by a member of the Radziwill family, which was related to the Elector Maximilian Emmanuel. In 1722, just about the time when the Schleissheim tapestries were delivered by De Vos, a member of the Radziwill family stayed for a month at the Elector's Court in Munich.[13]

XII. In Alexandria, Egypt, in the private collection of Mrs. Oswald Finney, is a group of six panels which belong to this general series and bear certain resemblances to the Dresden set of Augustus the Strong (No. I above). They consist of: *Campement ii*, *Fachinade ii*, *Embuscade ii*, *Pillage ii*, *La Marche ii*, and *Attacque* (influenced by the Blenheim *Oudenarde*). These all have trophy borders. With them is *La Halte*, which originally had a picture-frame border and belonged to another set.

The Plates show clearly enough, without any detailed explanations, the difference between the corresponding subjects of the earlier and the later series of designs. Various examples may differ in size, some subjects having been reduced or enlarged to suit individual requirements. One panel in which an actual variation may be noted is that from the Schleissheim Set which we have called *La Halte* (Fig. 60). The Drakelowe (Pourtalès) version (No. V) and the one sold at the Galerie Georges Petit (No. VIII) end on the right with figures driving off a horse behind a tree and a column of troops winding along a road into the distance. In the version from the Schleissheim Set, with the stitched-on borders from the Munich Set, the winding troops are the same, but the horse is stationary and in front of the tree. This variation is hardly sufficient to warrant our regarding the Schleissheim version as an older one, or including the subject in the early series in which it is not mentioned by name. Moreover, the figure of a soldier kneeling down to tie his shoe, on the extreme left, is an exact counterpart of one in the Blenheim Palace *Wynendael* (Fig. 46), which definitely points to a later origin. The galloping officer also is closely akin to the so-called Cadogan of *Bouchain III* (Fig. 52).

A curious link between the old and new series is to be traced in the case of *Fachinade*.

The Lumley Set, taken from the older designs, contains a variant form of this subject (Fig. 30), in which there is substituted for men chopping branches on the left of the picture a man wielding an axe, who appears in the new version at Drakelowe (Fig. 70) and in the Dresden Set. A pig which is to be seen in the left foreground of both *Pillage i* and *Pillage ii* (Figs. 13, 57), and also in the intervening Lumley Set (Fig. 32), is another detail linking all three versions together. Braquenie exhibited in Brussels in 1880[14] a piece described as 'Foragers of the Army of Louis XIV', which shows a trooper in his shirt-sleeves kneeling to rope a bundle of fodder, and behind him a standing figure with a scythe and another man carrying a bundle of hay (Fig. 71). The Braquenie panel may be an entrefenêtre like that of the first set of 1696 with a seated man smoking a pipe (Fig. 17)—a theme which appears in a different form in the Orkney and Cobham *Campement* panels (Figs. 27, 29). At any rate these variations suggest that Lambert de Hondt and his school had among their sketches other details and subjects which, not having been employed in their earlier compositions, could be embodied in subsequent versions of the *Art of War* for later patrons.

There still remains for consideration yet another set of military tapestries said to have been woven by Judocus de Vos from different cartoons traditionally attributed to Wouwerman. These panels hung in the Muschelsaal of the Rathaus in Cologne, for which they were bought in 1750. They have narrow picture-frame borders with shells in the angles and trophies in the centre at the top and bottom. This type of border was popular with De Vos and other weavers of the early eighteenth century. The subjects of the tapestries are:

71. *Fouragement* variant. Exhibited in Brussels in 1880 by the firm of Braquenie, Brussels.

Campement (Fig. 72), with the sutler's booth and the 'Poisoning of the Spy' scene.

Pillage; troops driving off sheep and cattle from a village.

La Marche; a long column of troops, wagons, and camp followers, winding through wooded and undulating country. On the wagons are crowned monograms apparently representing A.V.O. but this cannot yet be explained.

72. *Campement ii*, possibly woven by De Vos. Cologne Set. Formerly Cologne, Rathaus.

73. *Rencontre*, possibly woven by De Vos. Cologne Set. Formerly Cologne, Rathaus.

74. *Camp Life*, possibly woven by De Vos. Cologne Set. Formerly Cologne, Rathaus.

Fouragement; soldiers superintending hay being cut from stacks and loaded in barges or on pack-horses.

Rencontre (Fig. 73); a fierce cavalry action, one part of which centres round a horseman carrying a colour.

Camp Life (Fig. 74); troops resting in camp in improvised shelters, talking, drinking, cooking, smoking, and otherwise amusing themselves.

Replicas of *La Marche* and *Fouragement* (the former is in two pieces) are in the Hôtel de Ville at Hesdin, and of *La Marche* and *Rencontre* (neither complete) at Charlecote Park, near Stratford-upon-Avon.[15] The last two are supposed to have some connection with the Irish campaigns of William III, to which they obviously do not refer.

The importance of this set, which also is apparently intended to illustrate the *Art of War*, will be more clearly brought out in the discussion which follows of the general question of the authorship of the Blenheim and Schleissheim tapestries, which have in the past been connected, incorrectly, with the name of Van der Meulen.

CHAPTER VIII

LAMBERT DE HONDT

THE signatures on the Munich Set and the Baden Set prove that the designs for the *Art of War* series were the work of Lambert de Hondt and the document quoted by Wauters confirms the evidence.[1] This artist, who may thus be assumed to have been in the full tide of activity about 1690, may have been the son or nephew of another Lambert de Hondt who, to judge by a signed picture at Bamberg, flourished in 1636. The earlier Lambert de Hondt[2] is probably also the author of several other pictures, mostly battle scenes, in various galleries.

A painter active in 1636 could hardly have been the author of the *Art of War* about 1690, and consequently the artist of the cartoons with which we are concerned must be assumed to be a second and a younger Lambert de Hondt. An artist of this name was admitted to the painters' guild at Brussels in 1679, and was privileged in the same city in 1709—dates which would well agree with those of the *Art of War*. This Lambert de Hondt II may have been the painter of a picture at Frankfurt showing an attack on a convoy (Fig. 75). The windmill in the background, the galloping horses, and the rider flourishing a whip all resemble motives in the *Embuscade* of the *Art of War*. Again there are four pictures of cavalry combats, one at Dresden (Fig. 76), two at Schleissheim (one is illustrated as Fig. 77), and one in a dealer's possession, which all suggest the subject of *Rencontre* and consequently may perhaps be attributed to the second rather than to the first De Hondt.

There was also a Philip de Hondt, who is thought to have been a son or nephew of Lambert de Hondt II and who seems to have painted similar subjects. He was privileged in Brussels in 1711 and is again mentioned in 1735, but apparently died before 1743.* Although the history and relationships of the family are by no means clear and need further research, the evidence available seems to point to the existence of a group or school of artists principally of one family who specialized in the painting of military subjects.

To Lambert de Hondt II, on the ground of their strong stylistic likeness to the Munich Set, may also be attributed the designs for the panels at Hesdin and at Charlecote Park (see p. 111). The military subjects woven for the Duke of Marlborough and his

---

* At Rennes there is a picture of a naval battle the signature on which is variously said to be 'J de Hondt' or 'D de Hondt'. It might therefore have been brought into connexion with one of the family, but according to M. Ronnin the picture is unsigned, and it proves to differ in style from the military subjects which are usually associated with the name De Hondt.

75. Lambert de Hondt: *Attack on a Convoy*. Oil. Frankfurt, Staedel Institute.

Generals are adapted from his *Art of War* of 1696, and are thus based on his cartoons. The new and later Schleissheim version of the *Art of War* (Figs. 54–61) is a further adaptation of the original designs. Two of the subjects, *Fachinade* and *Attacque*, are combined, and *Rencontre* is omitted. To fill these two vacancies in the set of eight, two new subjects are introduced—*La Halte*, which contains several familiar motives, and the naval battle, *Sea Fight*. Some of the panels woven after the first *Art of War* for Marlborough and his Generals show the alterations beginning. The man wielding an axe in the Lumley *Fachinade* is the forerunner of a figure in the combined *Fachinade* and *Attacque* in the Schleissheim Set. One of the *Fouragement* pieces in the Lumley Set (Fig. 37) is a reversal of the Braquenie fragment (Fig. 71) and, as regards composition, stands midway between the Munich Set and the Schleissheim Set.

Then too, the Blenheim Palace 'Victories' (Figs. 40–51) are closely related to the Schleissheim Set for various reasons. First, the Schleissheim Set includes various excerpts from the Blenheim 'Victories', which were cynically furnished to the Elector Maximilian Emmanuel by the shrewd Flemings. Secondly, one panel of the Schleissheim

113

76. Lambert de Hondt: *Cavalry Combat*. Oil. Dresden, Picture Gallery.

Set, *La Halte*, has at least two motives which occur in the Blenheim 'Victories'—the soldier kneeling to tie his shoe from *Wynendael* and the galloping horseman from the third *Bouchain* panel. Lastly, the general likeness observable in the horses, the women and children, and the dogs, suggests that the designs for all these tapestries depend on the sketch-books of the same school, if not of the same artist. The Saxon Set formerly at Dresden (see p. 103), which consists of a variant of the *Hooghstet* panel at Blenheim and of four scenes from the Schleissheim Set, confirms the close connection which exists between the second version of the *Art of War* and the Blenheim 'Victories'. The sets of the first *Art of War*, and those woven for Marlborough and his Generals, were woven by Le Clerc and Van der Borcht; but the Blenheim Palace 'Victories', the whole Schleissheim Set, the Dresden Set, and various replicas related to them, all come from the looms of Judocus de Vos. Thus the successive stages of the development of the designs of the military tapestries—the *Art of War* and the Blenheim Palace 'Victories'— are all apparently connected with the first cartoons for the original series designed by Lambert de Hondt II before 1696.

77. Lambert de Hondt: *Cavalry Combat*. Oil. Schleissheim, Picture Gallery.

Lambert de Hondt was privileged in Brussels in 1709 and might therefore have taken part himself in redesigning his original *Art of War* of 1696 and in composing the 'Victories' of the Duke of Marlborough. By 1711, the earliest date at which these later designs are likely to have been completed, he would presumably have been advanced in years, and it would not be unreasonable to assume that Philip de Hondt and others of his school helped in the preparation of the cartoons, which would have been a considerable undertaking. This, as well as the later date, would easily account for any stylistic differences observable between the earlier and the later designs of the *Art of War*.

Before definitely adopting the view that Lambert de Hondt and his school were mainly responsible for the designs of the whole of this group of military tapestries, the claims of some other artists should first be considered. Prominent among battle painters of the period are Jan van Huchtenbergh and Adam van der Meulen. The former accompanied Prince Eugene on his campaigns and a series of paintings by him illustrating the victories of that great commander is in the gallery at Turin.[3] These, however, do not seem ever to have been used as cartoons for a set of tapestries, not even for the hypothetical series of the *Victories of Prince Eugene*, which is so often mentioned but seems never to have existed.[4] Van der Meulen, to whom the designs for the last *Art of War* are often attributed (see p. 111), is also an impossible candidate, for he died in 1690. It is improbable that either the set of Blenheim 'Victories' or the Schleissheim Set were designed before the autumn of 1711, the date of the fall of Bouchain, which figures so prominently in the Blenheim 'Victories', and Maximilian Emmanuel did not return to Munich until early in 1715. Further, Van der Meulen's artistic activity was almost entirely confined to France and his military tapestries to those woven at the Gobelins and at Beauvais to celebrate the virtues and victories of Louis XIV (see p. 19). In these, especially in the Beauvais series, the co-operation of Le Brun is obvious. Van der Meulen was a pupil of Snayers (1592–post 1669), who was at one time court painter to the Archduke Albert and designed the cartoons for the tapestries commemorating the exploits of that prince (cf. p. 14). With the exception of Martin, who was known as Martin des Batailles, Van der Meulen left no school or successors of any merit in France.

The designer of both Blenheim Sets and of the Schleissheim Set seems to have been acquainted with the work of Van der Meulen and also probably with that of Martin and the engravings of Sebastien le Clerc,[5] but does not seem to have been directly dependent on any of them. He was clearly an artist who delighted in drawing horses, had a good eye for geographical details as shown by his accuracy in the topography of the battle scenes, and was well versed in military matters. This character agrees with the style of Lambert de Hondt II, who designed the original cartoons of the *Art of War* about 1696, and so we reach the conclusion that it would not have been impossible for the cartoons of both Blenheim Sets and of the Schleissheim Set to have been drawn and adapted if not by Lambert de Hondt II then by his son or nephew Philip de Hondt and his school.

Still, in spite of the probability that all these military tapestries are intimately connected with Lambert de Hondt and his family and school, their stylistic kinship with Jan van Huchtenbergh and Van der Meulen suggests that behind them all is one common factor, an artist of the first rank.

Van Huchtenbergh is called by De Groot an imitator of Philips Wouwerman,[6] and Van der Meulen is said by some to have been a pupil of Wouwerman. In fact De Groot says that the latter, together with painters like Van der Meulen, set a fashion for the whole eighteenth century.[7] A white horse, which often occurs in the De Hondt designs, once used to be considered the hallmark of a painting by Wouwerman,[8] who also delighted in horses and scenes of camp life. It will be observed too that the grouping of the subjects of Wouwerman's pictures[9] at once suggests the eight subjects of De Hondt's *Art of War*. These comprise:

1. a series illustrating camp life or a sutler's booth,
2. scenes with woodcutters,
3. incidents of ambushes, such as robbers surprising travellers,
4. scenes of plundering,
5. troops on the march,
6. harvest scenes,
7. combats between bodies of cavalry.

The sutler's booth scene in the National Gallery known as 'La Belle Laitière' has a distinct suggestion of the *Campement* scenes, and similarly other Wouwerman pictures suggest the remainder. The second group parallels *Fachinade* and *Attacque*; the third *Embuscade*; the fourth *Pillage*; the fifth *La Marche*; the sixth *Fouragement*; and the last *Rencontre*.

The argument is strongly reinforced by an examination of the *Art of War* tapestries formerly hanging in Cologne (see pp. 109–11), which according to tradition are supposed to have been woven after designs by Wouwerman. In the *Campement* scene with the sutler's booth (Fig. 72), a favourite motive of the Wouwerman school, the group of a girl handing a glass or mug to a mounted man recurs. The trumpeter recalls the trumpeters in *Campement i* (Fig. 10) and *Campement ii* (Fig. 54), and the man drawing wine or beer from a barrel is a detail which occurs in *Campement ii*. The man in a cuirass seated on the right resembles a somewhat similar figure in *Campement i* and the party of soldiers watering their horses in a pond on the left repeats in a different form a detail from the same tapestry. Further, the officer on a white horse in the centre has a distinct likeness to the figure of the Duke of Marlborough in the *Donauwörth* and *Lines of Brabant* panels (Figs. 40, 43). The *Pillage* is reminiscent of both the first and second editions of this subject by De Hondt (Figs. 13, 57). In the *Fouragement* scene, the group of men loading hay onto pack-horses shows yet another version of this motive, which is seen both in *Fouragement i* and *Fouragement ii* (Figs. 15, 59). *The Rencontre* with the mêlée round a colour (Fig. 73) repeats the central theme of the De Hondt *Rencontre* (Fig. 21). The mounted officer with a raised sword on the left strongly suggests the mounted officer in *Embuscade i* (Fig. 12) and the horseman firing a pistol while bestriding his horse, which has been shot under him, occurs in *Embuscade ii* (Fig. 56). Lastly, the scene of *Camp Life* (Fig. 74) with soldiers resting and amusing themselves has reminiscences of both *Campement i* and *Campement ii*. It is obvious that the designs for this set of tapestries of the *Art of War*, whether their traditional attribution to Wouwerman is correct or not, are in any case clearly associated with those of De Hondt and seem to show the inspiration of the same sketch-books. They thus confirm the opinion, already put forward here, of a connection between Wouwerman and the school of De Hondt, which seems to have been very much under the influence of that master. In fact these tapestries form yet another link in the chain of evidence.

Thus, since Lambert de Hondt II seems to have been influenced by Wouwerman, it is by no means unlikely that he should have taken the essence of that master's subjects and crystallized them into a set of eight designs representing the *Art of War*. He obviously had not the same genius or inspiration as Wouwerman, but he was an artist of no mean skill, and clearly, owing to his facile style, eminently qualified to design tapestries. Wouwerman drew his military scenes from the Thirty Years War, and his very popularity with past generations proves his success as draughtsman and colourist. If he set a fashion which survived for the whole of the eighteenth century, it was in some measure due to his pupil or imitator Lambert de Hondt and his school, no less than to Van der Meulen, that the impulse he gave was so far-reaching. The change of taste and fashion has overlooked Lambert de Hondt, so that superficial connoisseurship has frequently given the work of his school to Van der Meulen, and the Brussels tapestries woven by that great craftsman Judocus de Vos to the Gobelins. The very fact that the work of these two masters De Hondt and De Vos has been usurped by Van der Meulen and the Gobelins is the clearest proof of its excellence.

Appendix I

THE UNWOVEN TAPESTRY OF RAMILLIES[1]

The drawing reproduced below (Fig. 78) is executed in Chinese ink and sepia on dull, greyish-blue paper with a watermark (see diagram), and it is what is technically known as a *petit patron* for a tapestry. That is to say it is the artist's preliminary sketch of the design of which the cartoon for the actual weaving of the tapestry would have been a full-scale enlargement. The drawing of the main subject, a battle scene, is complete, but that of the border is given only in part, as was the custom, because the right hand half of the border would naturally be a repetition of the left half.

The subject depicted is a pitched battle. On the left a desperate struggle between squadrons of charging horse is in progress, but the side led by an officer in armour in the left centre seems to be gaining the upper hand. In the foreground are fallen men and horses, and in the centre a dismounted man is running to the right. In the middle distance on the right, more of the cavalry action can be seen. The background shows the main setting of the whole battle reaching from *Franguinies* on the extreme left through *Ramilies, Offu,* and in front of *Bonmale.* Behind the last village in the distance on the extreme right, *Mont St. André, La Ramée Abb,* and *Jasselette* are visible.[2] All these

78. School of L. de Hondt: *Design for a tapestry of the Battle of Ramillies.* Ink and sepia drawing. Oslo, Kunstindustrimuseet.

places have their names, spelt thus, written just beside them. The border consists of trophies of arms and armour, standards and banners, drums, and military equipment of all kinds. In the centre of the upper border is a cartouche with a conventional view of a city labelled BRUSSEL and on its left on an oval shield is the lion of Brabant. In the lower border a similar view is labelled ANTWERPEN. In the two corners of the left border are ovals with conventional views of towns labelled MIENEN and DERMONDE[3] and other ovals in the corners of the right border are labelled GENDT and OSTENDE.

The battle depicted is without doubt that of Ramillies, fought on May 23rd, 1706, and the artist has taken as the moment of representation the crisis of the great combat between the French and the Allied horse on the left of the Allied line, when Marlborough himself twice charged at the head of reinforcements and in doing so nearly lost his life. These dramatic moments, which ended with the utter discomfiture of the French cavalry, decided the battle in favour of the Allies. The commander in armour seen in the forefront of the hottest part of the action is obviously Marlborough himself and the mêlée, which rages furiously round a standard, is probably intended to represent the gallant but fruitless efforts of the French *Maison du Roi* to rally round their colours and retrieve the fortunes of the day.[4] The overwhelming attack, with the whole force of Allied cavalry under the leadership of the Dutch Marshal Overkirk and of Marlborough himself, was so successful that it first of all crushed the right of Villeroy's line. Then the British and Dutch commanders, in spite of the efforts of Villeroy and the Elector Maximilian Emmanuel to form a second line, rolled up the whole French army from its right to its left, and the pressure of the Allied right centre and right then turned defeat into hopeless rout.

Villeroy and the Elector fled with the wreck of their army. Marlborough's pursuit was unrelenting. He entered Brussels in state on May 28th. Antwerp yielded to the Allies, and fortress after fortress opened its gates to the victors.

This brilliant victory, which drove the French out of Flanders, ought naturally to have been commemorated in the famous set of tapestries which Marlborough had woven for his palace at Blenheim, near Woodstock. This drawing is presumably the first sketch or *petit patron* for such a tapestry. It is curious, however, that Ramillies alone of Marlborough's victories is unrepresented in that famous series of tapestries immortalizing his triumphs, which adorn the state rooms at Blenheim.

This *petit patron* for a Ramillies panel shows the same method as the *Hooghstet (Blenheim)* tapestry of commemorating, by the use of ovals in the border, the capture of towns which yielded after the victory (cf. Fig. 42), and the proportions of the drawing seem to indicate that the resulting tapestry would have been of approximately the same size as the *Hooghstet* panel. In short the drawing appears to have been designed for a tapestry which would have been the ideal pendant to the *Hooghstet* tapestry.

A Ramillies tapestry is hardly likely to have been designed for anyone but Marl-borough himself. We can assume then that the designer intended a Ramillies tapestry, of which this is the *petit patron*, to be one of the series at Blenheim and indeed the correspondence of the border with those of the Blenheim 'Victories', especially the *Hooghstet* panel, in shape, style, and subject, leaves little room, if any, for serious doubt. Thus the design would in all probability be the work of the same artist or the same school.

There is every reason to believe that the school or family of De Hondt was responsible for the designs of the Blenheim 'Victories' (see pp. 113–4) and indeed close analysis of their composition and comparison of them with the De Hondt military tapestries shows that they all belong to the same school. It would be rash, of course, to assert that Lambert de Hondt or some other definite member of the family drew the *petits patrons* for them, but it is quite reasonable to suggest that one of the De Hondt family or school was their author. Thus in the Ramillies *petit patron* we should expect to find the same characteristics and style. The Blenheim 'Victories', for instance the *Lines of Brabant*, are distinguished by faithful delineation of the topographical features of the battlefield. Here too the Ramillies *petit patron* follows the others, and the topography of the battle-field with the indication and names of the villages and with the emphasis laid on the great cavalry action on the Allied left wing shows that the artist was familiar both with the ground and with the actual details of the battle. In the incidents of the drawing it is noticeable that the horses are extremely prominent and are treated with sympathy and understanding. In the military tapestries by De Hondt himself and in those of his school, great care and attention is paid to the horses throughout. In general composition, the desperate fight round the colour in the Ramillies *petit patron* recalls the mêlée round a standard in the *Rencontre* of De Hondt's *Art of War* of 1696 (Fig. 21). Further, the dismounted man in the right centre who is running off suggests the man in the *Embuscade* of the same period (Fig. 12) who is dashing away from the trapped convoy and its escort. Although no specific likeness is observable, the fallen or falling trooper and horses also display a general resemblance to those in the two panels just mentioned of the *Art of War* of 1696—*Rencontre* and *Embuscade*. Again pictures of cavalry actions by Lambert de Hondt in the galleries at Dresden (Fig. 76) and at Schleissheim (Fig. 77) show considerable likeness to the Ramillies *petit patron*. The charging squadrons, the troopers firing pistols or cutting at one another, and the fallen men and horses, are details which occur both in the pictures and in the *petit patron*. It is possible, therefore, to say that the Ramillies drawing can be attributed to the same school as the other Blenheim 'Victories'—that is to say to the school of De Hondt.

One other point remains for discussion. Why was no Ramillies tapestry woven for the series of the Blenheim Palace 'Victories'? It has been suggested earlier (see p. 44) that on his triumphal entry into the city of Brussels on May 28th, 1706, after the battle fought on May 23rd, the city may have resolved to present Marlborough with tapestry to celebrate the victory, and that the gift may have been the set of the *Art of War* which is now at Blenheim Palace (Figs. 22–26). If this were so, it would account for the greater richness of this set of tapestries (see App. IV, C). Burgomaster Max of Brussels in the 1930s, at the request of Earl Granville, then British Ambassador, kindly had the archives searched to see whether there was any record of such a presentation to Marlborough, but the only incident of the period discovered was the provision of wine by the city for the table of General Charles Churchill, whom his brother had made military governor of Brussels after Ramillies.

The absence of any record of such a gift is not decisive against it, for the evidence is after all only negative. In any case, if the suggestion is right it would appear that the city of Brussels, instead of having a special cartoon of the actual Battle of Ramillies prepared, ordered a set of the *Art of War* of 1696 as the most appropriate gift for the great commander who had just shown how fully he possessed that art.

What probably happened was this. At the end of the war, after 1711 (the date of Bouchain), if, as seems probable, Marlborough then completed his order from De Vos for a set of tapestries to commemorate his victories, the artist called upon to design it would naturally have included Ramillies in his set of *petits patrons*. Marlborough, knowing that Brussels was presenting him with tapestry to commemorate Ramillies and not realizing that it would represent the *Art of War* rather than the actual battle, decided in consequence that no Ramillies panel should be woven for his own set. Marlborough was by nature frugal, knew well the value of money, and disliked unnecessary expenditure. He would therefore regard the promised Brussels gift of tapestry as an economy inasmuch as it saved him from having a Ramillies woven at his own expense.

This seems the most rational explanation of the absence of a Ramillies from the Blenheim 'Victories' and explains also the greater richness of the five panels of the *Art of War* at Blenheim, because they were a gift from the city of Brussels. Thus, with Ramillies excluded from the 'Victories', the *petit patron* was separated from the rest (which would have been enlarged into full cartoons and remained in De Vos's atelier). It wandered about the world as an isolated drawing rejected from the purpose for which its artist designed it, and finally reached an art dealer's in Stockholm. Here it was recognized by the keen eye of the late Dr. John Böttiger, Intendant of the Royal Swedish Collections. On his recommendation it was purchased for Kunstindustrimuseet in Oslo and its presence there supports the suggestions just put forward. Its discovery and analysis provide a reasonable and plausible explanation for the omission of Ramillies from the famous set of 'Victories' in Blenheim Palace.

Appendix II

ANALYSIS OF SETS OF THE 'ART OF WAR'

		Pages	Figures

1. *Art of War*: First Version. A set of theoretical, stylized incidents of contemporary warfare, based on the first version of Lambert de Hondt's *Art of War*. Woven by Le Clerc and Van der Borcht.

			Pages	Figures
(a) 1696 (delivered)	Munich Set (woven for the Elector Maximilian Emmanuel of Bavaria)		29–39	10–16
	Baden Set (woven for the Margrave Louis of Baden)		39–40	20–21
	William III (?) Set		40–42	
	Lisbon Set		42	
(b) 1706 (?)	First Blenheim Palace Set (woven for the Duke of Marlborough)		44–49	22–26
(c) *c.* 1706–12	Sets woven for Marlborough's Generals		49–59	27–38
	Cobham Argyll Lumley			
	Cadogan Orkney Webb			

2. *Blenheim Palace 'Victories'*. A fresh and original series of tapestries, designed by Lambert de Hondt, which depict with great accuracy of detail the actual campaigns of the Duke of Marlborough, using occasional motives from the *Art of War*. Woven by Judocus de Vos. About 1712–17.   60–89   40–52

3. *Art of War*: Second Version. Tapestries based on the second version of Lambert de Hondt's *Art of War*, which contains adaptations of the first version (with details often reused or reversed) and excerpts from the Blenheim Palace 'Victories'. Woven by Judocus de Vos.

			Pages	Figures
(a) *c.* 1724	Schleissheim Set (woven for the Elector Maximilian Emmanuel of Bavaria)		90–102	54–67
	Archbishop Clemens August Set		102–103	
(b) *c.* 1724	Other sets:			
	I. Dresden (Augustus the Strong, King of Saxony)		103	(69)
	II. Schloss Ivenack, Mecklenburg		106	
	III. Schloss Neudeck, Upper Silesia		106	
	IV. Brussels (a) Banque de Belgique		106	
	(b) Braquenie panel		109	
	V. Drakelowe (Sir Robert Gresley) (Pourtalès)		106	68, 70
	VI. Calehill Park (Sir Chester Beatty)		106	
	VII. Sir Philip Sassoon (formerly property of Lord Brassey)		106	
	VIII. San Diego, California (Fine Arts Gallery)		107	
	IX. Paris, Petit Palais (Collection Dutuit)		108	
	X. Paris, Founès		108	
	XI. Vilna, Cathedral		108	
	XII. Alexandria, Egypt (Mrs. Oswald Finney)		108	

Appendix III

ANALYSIS OF SUBJECTS OF THE 'ART OF WAR'

The tables below show all known extant examples of the subjects of the two versions of the *Art of War* tapestries.

The roman numerals and letters in the first table refer to Plates I–VI (pages 125–30), where the panels are grouped according to subject for easy comparison. The arabic numerals in the second table refer to illustrations in the main text. The diamond shapes in both tables indicate tapestries which it has not been possible to illustrate.

FIRST VERSION

	1. Campement	2. Fachinade	3. Embuscade	4. Pillage	5. La Marche	6. Fouragement	7. Attacque	8. Rencontre
(a) Munich Set	Ia	IIa	IIId	IId	IVa	IVe	Vd	
Baden Set	Ib	IIb	IIIe	IIe			Ve	VIa
William III(?) Set	Ic				IVc			VIc
Lisbon Set		◇		◇	◇			◇
(b) Blenheim Set	Id			IIIa, b			Vf	VIb
(c) Orkney Set	If		IIIf		IVb		Vg	
Cobham Set	Ie		IIIg			Va	Vh	
Lumley Set	Ig	IIc	IIIc	IIf, g	IVd	Vb, c		VId

SECOND VERSION

	1. Campment ii	2. Fachinade ii	3. Embuscade ii	4. Pillage ii	5. La Marche ii	6. Fouragement ii	7. La Halte	8. Sea Fight
(a) Schleissheim Set	54	55	56	57	58	59	60	61
(b) Other sets:								
I. Dresden	◇	◇			◇		◇	
II. Ivenack	◇				◇		◇	◇
III. Neudeck					◇			
IV. Brussels	◇			◇		◇		◇
V. Drakelowe		70		68			◇	
VI. Calehill					◇			
VII. Sassoon	◇				◇			
VIII. San Diego				◇			(◇)	
IX. Paris (Dutuit)	◇							
X. Paris (Founès)	◇							
XI. Vilna					◇			
XII. Alexandria	◇	◇	◇	◇	◇		◇	

a. Munich *Campement*

b. Baden *Campement*

c. Founès *Campement*

d. Blenheim *Campement*

e. Cobham *Campement*

Orkney *Campement*

g. Lumley *Campement*

Plate I. *Campement*

a. Munich *Fachinade*

d. Munich *Pillage*

b. Baden *Fachinade*

e. Baden *Pillage*

c. Lumley *Fachinade*

f. Lumley *Pillage* (left)

g. Lumley *Pillage* (right)

Plate II. *Fachinade* and *Pillage*

a, b. Blenheim *Pillage* (centre and right)   c. Lumley *Embuscade*

d. Munich *Embuscade*   e. Baden *Embuscade*

f. Orkney *Embuscade*   g. Cobham *Embuscade*

Plate III. *Pillage* and *Embuscade*

a. Munich *La Marche*

b. Orkney *La Marche*

c. Founès *La Marche*

d. Lumley *La Marche*

e. Munich *Fouragement*

Plate IV. *La Marche* and *Fouragement*

a. Cobham *Fouragement*

b. Lumley *Fouragement* (centre)

c. Lumley *Fouragement* (right)

d. Munich *Attacque*

e. Baden *Attacque*

f. Blenheim *Attacque*

g. Orkney *Attacque*

h. Cobham *Attacque*

Plate V. *Fouragement* and *Attacque*

a. Baden *Rencontre*

b. Blenheim *Rencontre*

c. Founès *Rencontre*

d. Lumley *Rencontre*

Plate VI. *Rencontre*

Appendix IV

NOTES FROM THE BLENHEIM ARCHIVES

These excerpts from the Blenheim Palace archives were not available to the author. They are vivid and interesting in themselves but unfortunately they give little information exact enough for use in identifying the sets discussed in this monograph. The most definite comments obviously concern the tapestries known as the *Alexander Set*, woven for the private apartments (Bedchamber and Anteroom) of Sarah and John. That they are known to have been woven by De Vos and bear the same arms as the two military sets tends to add to the confusion rather than to the clarification of our dating problem.

   These notes are reproduced with the kind permission of the Duke of Marlborough and of Mr. David Green.

I. CORRESPONDENCE ETC. CONCERNING THE TAPESTRIES

A. John Duke of Marlborough to Sarah Duchess of Marlborough. The Hague 19 December, 1704
. . . *The hangings I bring you having been thrown into a little river I was obliged to open them but they receiv'd no damadge. They will please you for they are fine & very agreeable but they are too deep for any of your rooms. I shall also bring with me a great provision of Giniper Watter for your and Lord Treasurer . . .* (Blen. E 2)

B. John to Sarah. Velaine 13 September, 1706
. . . *I am told of a Sute of Hangings that is at Antwerp that may be bought for eighteen hundred pounds & that they are worth much more. Wou'd you have mee bye them? They have neither silver nor gold in them nor were ever us'd. They were bespoke by the late King . . .* (Blen. E 3)

C. John to Sarah. 1 November, 1706
. . . *The hangings I had made att Bruxelles are finish'd and the greatest fault I find with them is their having so much silver & gold in them. However I hope you will like them. If I had receiv'd the measures of the apartment you & I are to live in I should have bespoke some more, but now you may see these & be the better able to tell me what alterations you will have made in the next & I believe you will be of my opinion to have no silver nor gold . . .*
(Blen. E 3)

D. John to Sarah. Osnebourg 7 April, 1707
. . . *Pray lett me have the measures of the Hangings which I am to bespeak for your & my apartement . . .* (Blen. E 3)

E. John to Sarah. Meldert 7 July, 1707
. . . *I shall write about the hangings & I hope there is time enough to make them of the hight you desire . . .*
(Blen. E 3)

F. John to Sarah. Bruxelles 14 May, 1708
. . . *I have been to see the hangings for your apartment & mine. As much as are done of them I think are very fine. I shall not send them over till the winter unless you desire them. I shall be glad at your leasure you would be providing every thing that may be necessary for furnishing those two apartments . . .* (Blen. E 4)

His Grace the Duke of Marlboroughs Account to 30th June, 1708 June 14 Paid Mr. Dolben for Embroideries for a Bed & 3 Peices of Tapestry Hangings for Woodstock £225. (Blen. XXIII)

G. John to Sarah. 11 July, 1709
. . . *I am desirous that you would send the exact measures of the roomes in your house in London* [Marlborough House] *which you desier should be furnish'd with Tapistry.*
(Blen. E 4)

H. John to Sarah. Ghent (?) 24 June, 1709
. . . *the 2 suttes of hangings which were made at Bruxelles by Vanbroukes measures cost me about 800 pounds, so that if possible they should serve for the roomes they were intended for, being sure in England there can bee none so good & fine . . .* (Blen. E 4)

I. John to Sarah. The Hague 19 March, 1710
. . . *I also send you my Coat of Armes as they are to be on the hangings now makeing at Bruxelles, so that I desire you*

131

will send for Vanderberg & that hee should take care that the Crown & Armes in the hangings already come over bee exact as this is . . . (Blen. E 4)

J. John to Sarah. The Hague (?) 10 July, 1710
. . . The Tapistry man of Bruxelles has been with me & asures me that I shall bring you over the hangings for your bed chamber & the room before itt . . . (Blen. E 5)

K. John to Sarah. Maestricht 5 February, 1713
. . . When you go by Bruxelles I desire you would give your self the trouble of going to see the Hangings at Monsr. De Vost. You may do it in half an hour whielst they get the dinner ready . . . (Blen. E 5)

L. Sarah to Lord Cadogan. 26 August, 1717
. . . I understand by Hodges, after your Lordship left Tunbridge, that there is mony Due for hangings which were to have come with the King, & for Wine. Whenever you please to let me have that account I will be sure to write to Mr Clifford that it may be paid out of the Duke of Marlboroughs mony. I hope there was some bargain made with the Tapistry Man that he might not impose as most of those people are apt to do. But when he is not left to him self I know hee has sold the same Designs at very reasonable prices . . . (Blen. E XII (39))

II. TAPESTRY DOCUMENTS
(quoted, with his kind permission, from David Green's *Blenheim Palace*, p. 248)

'The Tapestry Contract, in French, is among the Blenheim archives (A–II–35), with a letter from Cardonnel [the Duke's Secretary] (September 12, 1707) in which he makes it clear that *in case the*

Hangings when made are not approv'd and accepted by his Grace, the sume paid in advance shall be returned.

'A portfolio in the Long Library contains de Vos' bills and estimates. All the tapestries were to be in frames, and they were to include the story of Alexander (this set now hangs in the Duchess's Bedchamber). Above a bold and characterful signature de Vos writes (December 4, 1715): *J'ai l'honneur de mander à Votre Alteze que Ses Tapisseries sont achevées et en toute perfection au grand étonnement et satisfaction de tout ceux de cette Science qui les ont vues.* Two years later he refers to his tapestry of the passage of the lines above Louvain as one of the finest pieces he had ever made.'

III. SARAH'S INVENTORY OF 1740

A List of the Tapestry Hangings that are at Blenheim:
In the Dutchess of Marlboroughs Bedchamber a very fine suit I dont know the Story.
In the Bow Window Room Tapestry Hangings of Alexander's Battles.
In the Dukes Dressing Room a suit of Alexander's Battles.
In the Dukes Bedchamber Tapestry Hangings—Alexander's Battles.
In the Grand Bedchamber—Tapestry Hangings of Battles.
In the great room beyond that—Tapestry Hangings of Battles.
In the Apartment next the Salon west—two very fine suits of Tapestry Hangings of Battles and Seiges.
8 Suits of the fine hangings on that floor, all as fresh as new.

NOTES

I. EARLY MILITARY TAPESTRIES (pp. 11–12)

1. See Marillier, *Burlington Magazine*, vol. XLVI, p. 36; Hunter, *The Practical Book of Tapestries*, p. 73. The most complete existing set is at Zamora, see A. Gómez Martínez and B. Chillón Sampedro, *Los Tapices de la Catedral de Zamora*, Plates 7–10. One panel formerly in the Château de Bayard is in the Victoria and Albert Museum, see *Catalogue of Tapestries*, p. 25.

2. Kurth, *Jahrbuch der kunsthistorischen Sammlungen*, vol. XXXIV, p. 96. Henry VII bought in 1488 a *History of Troy* series from John Grenier of Tournai, see Thomson, *Tapestry Weaving in England*, p. 19.

3. P. Schumann, *Der Trojanische Krieg*.

4. Jubinal, *Tapisseries historiées*, vol. II, Berne, Plates 5–10; Kurth, op. cit., p. 80; Hunter, op. cit., p. 89.

5. The *Sack of Jerusalem* series should perhaps be described more properly as the *Vengeance of the Lord*. Several fragments from at least three different sets exist in different collections and are widely scattered, see Hunter, op. cit., p. 51; but

to his list should be added three more pieces in the church of Notre-Dame de Nantilly at Saumur and one in the Bargello at Florence.

6. Kurth, op. cit., p. 77, Fig. 13. It was acquired by the Musée du Cinquantenaire at Brussels from the Somzée Collection at the sale in May 1901. The hero *Rolant* with his sword *durendal* appears no less than five times in the tapestry.

7. Kurth, op. cit., p. 101, Fig. 32. The three fragments of this panel came from the Édouard Aynard Collection sold in Paris on December 4th, 1913.

8. Kurth, op. cit., p. 71, Plates VII, VIII; Popham, *Burlington Magazine*, vol. XLV, pp. 60–6.

9. Loriquet, *Tapisseries de la Cathédrale de Reims*, p. 43 ff., two plates.

10. Kurth, op. cit., p. 78, Fig. 10.

11. Laborde, *Les Ducs de Bourgogne*, vol. II, p. 271, No. 4285.

12. Göbel, *Wandteppiche*, pt. I, p. 237.

13. Dos Santos, *As Tapeçarias da Tomada de Arzila*.

II. THE RENAISSANCE (pp. 13–18)

1. Pinchart, *Histoire générale de la Tapisserie*, vol. III (Pays-Bas), Plate 86.

2. Jubinal, *Tapisseries historiées*, vol. I, Dijon, Plates 1–3.

3. Göbel, *Wandteppiche*, pt. I, p. 415, Plates 375, 376.

4. Göbel, op. cit., pt. I, p. 414, Plates 51, 70, 71, 184, 276.

5. Wauters, *Bernard van Orley*, pp. 64–73.

6. Houdoy, *Tapisseries représentant la Conquête du Royaulme de Thunes*; Valencia de Don Juan, *Tapices de la Corona de España*, vol. I, Plates 56–65; Calvert, *The Spanish Royal Tapestries*, p. 32 ff., Plates 35–43; Göbel, op. cit., pt. II, p. 475; *Wiener Gobelins Sammlung*, Plates 81–90; Birk, *Jahrbuch der kunsthistorischen Sammlungen*, vol. I, p. 224; Engerth, ibid., vol. II, p. 145; vol. IX, p. 419; vol. XI, p. 113.

   There were other sets of the *Conquest of Tunis* in existence, as appears from the discovery, by

Marshal de Coutades, of a panel combining Nos. 7 and 8 of the original series, at a castle in Mechlin during the Seven Years War. Schmitz (*Bildteppiche*, 3rd ed., p. 238) mentions a set woven by Pannemaker for Cardinal Granvella, part of which is now in the Château Montgeoffroy.

7. *Mémoires de Feld-Maréchal Comte de Mérode-Westerloo*, vol. II, pp. 74, 75.

8. This was a common error; cf. Göbel, op. cit., pt. I, p. 426.

9. Engerth (op. cit., vol. II, p. 147) suggested that the cartoons had remained in Brussels up to the time that De Vos made use of them, but the above incident clearly proves this not to have been the case.

10. Miss Phyllis Ackermann (*Tapestries illustrating Scenes from the War of the Spanish Succession*, p. 12) by an anachronism says that Vermeyen (d. 1559) introduced into one cartoon the portrait of De

Vos, who flourished in the first quarter of the eighteenth century. She has misunderstood Göbel's remark (op. cit., pt. I, p. 393).

11. Göbel, op. cit., pt. I, p. 334, Plate 281; Calvert, *Spanish Royal Tapestries*, Plates 176–80.
12. They were catalogued in the Berwick and Alba sale of 1877, but not sold. Göbel, op. cit., pt. I, p. 312.
13. Shown at the Flemish Exhibition, Burlington House, 1927; Göbel, op. cit., pt. I, p. 547, Plate 499.
14. Göbel, op. cit., pt. II, p. 351; cf. Fenaille, *Tapisseries des Gobelins*, vol. I, p. 257 ff.
15. The *Jarnac* panel came to light at the sale of Baron Pichon's collection in 1897, when it passed

into the possession of the Vicomte de Reiset. On the sale of the latter's collection in 1922, the panel was acquired for the Louvre.

16. Göbel, op. cit., pt. I, p. 558.
17. Göbel, op. cit., pt. I, p. 560, Plate 507.
18. Göbel, op. cit., pt. I, p. 539, Plate 490.
19. Göbel, op. cit., pt. I, p. 540; Thomson, *Tapestry Weaving in England*, p. 33.
20. Barnard and Wace, *Archaeologia*, vol. LXXVIII, p. 289.
21. Mayer, *Geschichte der Wandteppichfabriken*, p. 31.
22. Mayer, op. cit., p. 44 ff. Another set was subsequently woven in Paris from the same cartoons by the factory of Van der Planken and Comans, Göbel, *Pantheon*, vol. V, p. 153 ff.

III. THE REIGN OF LOUIS XIV (pp. 19–28)

1. Fenaille, *Tapisseries des Gobelins*, vol. II, p. 99 ff.
2. Göbel, *Wandteppiche*, pt. II, p. 216.
3. Two panels bear the Tournai mark and the signature of P. Béhagle.
4. Schmitz, *Bildteppiche*, 3rd ed., p. 166, Fig. 87.
5. Göbel, op. cit., pt. I, p. 543.
6. Böttiger, *Svenska Statens Samling af Väfda Tapeter*, vol. II, p. 81.
7. Liisberg, *Rosenborg*, pp. 130–7; cf. Müntz, *A Short History of Tapestry*, p. 306; Müntz, *Histoire générale de la Tapisserie*, vol. II (Le Danemark, etc.), p. 28; Göbel, *Cicerone*, 1926, p. 703.
8. Boesen, *Christian den Femtes Rosenborgtapeter fra den skaanske krig*, passim.
9. Böttiger, op. cit., vol. II, p. 81, Plates XXIX-XXXII.
10. 'Lord Iveagh's Solebay Tapestries', *Country Life*, vol. LXV, pp. 351–3; see also the correspondence

in *The Times* during October 1925, and Thomson, *Tapestry Weaving in England*, p. 104.

11. Marillier, *English Tapestries of the Eighteenth Century*, p. xiii.
12. *Country Life*, vol. LXV, p. 352, Fig. 4.
13. *Country Life*, vol. LXV, p. 352, Fig. 5.
14. These three from Sir Gerald Codrington's collection were sold at Christie's on July 12th, 1923, and may be the three panels in private possession mentioned by Mr. Law, *The Times*, October 29th, 1925.
15. Thomson, op. cit., p. 105, Fig. 32.
16. Thomson, op. cit., p. 106, Fig. 33.
17. *Country Life*, vol. LXV, p. 351, Fig. 1; p. 352, Fig. 3; p. 351, Fig. 2.
18. Göbel, *Wandteppiche*, pt. II, p. 361 ff.
19. Göbel, op. cit., pt. I, p. 353, Plate 298.

IV. DE HONDT'S 'ART OF WAR' OF 1696 (pp. 29–42)

1. *Archives Nationales*, Paris, T. 153 40/41, Cotte 158.
2. Siegel, *Die Flagge*, p. 161, Plate 32.
3. Göbel, *Wandteppiche*, pt. I, Plate 329.
4. Geherig, *Kunstchronik*, vol. XXXIII (1921–2), p. 98.
5. Rott, *Badische Heimat*, vol. IX (1922), pp. 6, 8, 71.
6. Shown in 1953, as Catalogue No. 48, in an exhibition 'Bildteppiche aus 6 Jahrhunderten' in the Museum für Kunst und Gewerbe, Hamburg.

7. Wauters, *Bulletin des Commissions Royales d'Art et d'Archéologie*, vol. XVI (1877), p. 324.
8. Wauters, op. cit., p. 325.
9. There are tapestries representing the *Battle of the Boyne* and the *Siege of Londonderry* in the Bank of Ireland, formerly the Irish House of Parliament, in Dublin; but these were woven in Ireland by one Robert Baillie between 1730 and 1734 and have no connection with the Flemish set; Thom-

son, *Tapestry Weaving in England*, p. 152; National Museum of Science and Art, Dublin, *Museum Bulletin*, vol. IV (1914), pt. I, p. 2 ff., Plates IV, V.

10. A *Rencontre* panel was sold by Parke-Bernet in New York on April 15th, 1961 (Sale 2031, Lot 363) and bought by a New York private collector. It has no frame and is almost identical with the Founès panel.

11. *Boletim dos Museus Nacionais de Arte Antiga*, vol. I, 1935, p. vii ff.; vol. II, 1942, No. 7, Figs. 7, 8, 9.

V. MARLBOROUGH AND HIS GENERALS (pp. 43–59)

1. Three sets of tapestries were presented to Marshal Saxe by the City of Brussels, Göbel, *Wandteppiche*, pt. I, p. 353.
2. See *Connoisseur*, vol. LXI (October 1921), p. 110.
3. This was in the possession of Moss Harris.
4. *Campement* was Lot 121b and *Attacque* (called *Fachinade* in the catalogue) was Lot 121a in the sale at Sotheby's on 25th October 1963.
5. General Henry Lumley, who fought at Blenheim, Ramillies, and Oudenarde, and predeceased his father in 1710. The father was succeeded by his second son Richard in 1721.

VI. THE BLENHEIM PALACE 'VICTORIES' (pp. 60–89)

1. He was also a great weaver of Teniers subjects.
2. Fortescue, *A History of the British Army*, passim.

VII. OTHER CONTEMPORARY TAPESTRIES (pp. 90–111)

1. It is marked FT. A MUNICH. 1724. Maximilian Emmanuel restarted the tapestry works at Munich in 1718 under four French weavers. They were actively continued by his successors Charles Albert and Maximilian Joseph, who had a set of ten tapestries woven during the years 1735–46 and 1750–65 representing the *History of the Dukes of Bavaria*. Six of them are battle subjects, dealing with events of the thirteenth and fifteenth centuries. See Mayer, op. cit., p. 58 ff.
2. Kürköln, Erzbischöfe, Clemens August, No. 19, 359 fol. ausg. 27.9.18, *Documentum Notariale super facta Inventarisatione deren in hiesiger Residenz befindlichen Meublen und Effecten*, folios 68–70; cf. Renard, *Bonner Jahrbücher*, vol. C, p. 52.
3. Renard, op. cit., vol. XCIX, p. 173.
4. Phyllis Ackermann, *Tapestries illustrating Scenes from the War of the Spanish Succession* (a Margraf brochure): cf. Saxe, *International Studio*, vol. 87 (August 1927), p. 74. All five panels were shown by Margraf at the Philadelphia Sesquicentennial Exhibition in 1926.
5. Miss Ackermann, however, incorrectly identifies it as the meeting of Marlborough and Prince Eugene with the Margrave of Baden at the Neckar in June 1704, the Margrave apparently being represented by the figure of Marshal Tallard in the act of surrender, and Eugene by one of the English officers serving as his escort. The weaver has done some strange things with the Duke of Marlborough's cartoons, as we have seen, but there really appears to be no reason for this particular perversion. Miss Ackermann's difficulty was probably one of dates. The Dresden tapestries are said by Professor Hermann Schmitz (*Bildteppiche*, 3rd ed., p. 256) to have been acquired in 1708, and unfortunately one of the other pieces was once known as Malplaquet, although the Battle of Malplaquet was not fought until 1709. This would not necessarily affect an incident of 1704, but having to give up one ascription she doubtless decided to give up both, not knowing the Blenheim designs. The date given is manifestly impossible, and the Dresden archivist who has obligingly made a search cannot either confirm it or trace its origin. It may be a slip for 1718; but in any case, as the Blenheim tapestries are probably later than the capture of Bouchain in 1711, and replicas must be later still, no date earlier than 1712 need seriously be

considered. In the second place the panel called *Malplaquet* has nothing to do with that battle.

6. Sold on February 14th, 1964 (Lot 22), to a London dealer.
7. Keuller–Wauters, *Tapisseries historiées à l'Exposition Nationale Belge de 1880*, Plates 101–3.
8. Göbel, *Wandteppiche*, pt. 1, Plate 297.
9. See *Nationalmuseets Utställningsblad*, No. 3, 1918, where it is described as a Gobelins tapestry after Van der Meulen, representing Louis XIV on horseback with his staff.
10. January 8th, 1927, p. 4; cf. *Art and Archaeology*, vol. XXVII, p. 212.
11. His real name was Adam and not Anton Frans.
12. Morelowski, *Gobelinz Wilénskie*, Fig. 16, p. 73.
13. Kotłubaj, *Galerie des portraits des Radziwill*, p. 437.
14. Keuller–Wauters, op. cit., Plate 100.
15. *Country Life*, vol. I (1897), p. 46 and pp. 78–80: vol. XXXV (1914) has another article on Charlecote, in which the tapestries are illustrated (pp. 126–34).

VIII. LAMBERT DE HONDT (pp. 112–118)

1. Wauters, *Bulletin des Commissions Royales d'Art et d'Archéologie*, vol. XVI, p. 324.
2. For the careers of the various De Hondts see Thieme-Becker.
3. They are engraved in *Batailles gagnées par le . . . Prince Fr. Eugene de Savoye . . . gravées par le Sr. Jean Huchtenburg avec des explications Historiques par Mr. J. Du-Mont*, La Haye, 1725.
4. Wauters, op. cit., vol. XVII, p. 162, appears to give as authority for the existence of this set the passage from the memoirs of Count Mérode-Westerloo, already mentioned (see p. 14 and note). This passage, however, refers to the *Conquest of Tunis* set woven by De Vos, which Wauters mentions on the same page, so that it is clear that his reference has been misplaced by a printer's error.
5. E.g. the series called 'Les petites conquêtes du Roi', Jombert, *Catalogue raisonné de l'œuvre de S. Leclerc*, vol. II, p. 147; cf. Guiffrey–Marcel, *Inventaire général*, vol. VIII, Nos. 8557–8566.
6. Hofstede de Groot, *Catalogue raisonné of the works of the most eminent Dutch painters*, vol. II, p. 253.
7. Hofstede de Groot, op. cit., p. 254.
8. Hofstede de Groot, op. cit., p. 251.
9. Hofstede de Groot, op. cit., p. 255 ff.

Appendix I

THE UNWOVEN TAPESTRY OF RAMILLIES (pp. 119–122)

1. This is adapted, with the kind permission of Kunstindustrimuseet, Oslo, from A. J. B. Wace, 'The unwoven tapestry of Ramillies', Oslo, Kunstindustrimuseet Årbok, 1935, 6, 7.
2. All these places are given in the plan of the Battle of Ramillies in *Carte des Pays Bas*, published by H. Fricx, Brussels, 1712, Plate 29.
3. Miss G. T. van Ysselsteyn has called attention to the fact that this spelling of the names suggests the Brabant dialect, especially that of Antwerp.
4. For this and other details of the battle, see Winston Churchill, *Marlborough: His Life and Times*, vol. III, p. 113 ff. ; also George Macaulay Trevelyan, *England under Queen Anne: Ramillies*.

SELECT BIBLIOGRAPHY

Books and Periodicals

Barnard, see Wace.

Birk, Ernst von, 'Inventar der im Besitze des Aller-höchsten Kaiserhauses befindlichen Niederländer Tapeten und Gobelins', *Jahrbuch der kunsthisto-rischen Sammlungen des Allerhöchsten Kaiserhauses*, vol. I (Vienna, 1883), pp. 213–48.

Boesen, Gudmund, *Christian den Femtes Rosenborg-tapeter fra den skaanske krig*, Copenhagen, 1949.

Böttiger, John, *Svenska Statens Samling af Väfda Tapeter*, Stockholm, 1895–6 (vol. 2).

Calvert, A. F., *The Spanish Royal Tapestries*, London, John Lane, 1921.

Churchill, Sir Winston, *Marlborough: His Life and Times*, London, Harrap, 1933–8.

Crooke y Navarrot, see Valencia de Don Juan.

Dos Santos, Reynaldo, *As Tapeçarias da Tomada de Arzila*, Lisbon, 1925.

Dumont, J., *Batailles gagnées par le . . . Prince Fr. Eugene de Savoye etc.: dépeintes et gravées . . . par . . . Jean Huchtenberg, avec des explications Historiques par Mr. J. Du-Mont*, La Haye, 1725.

Engerth, Eduard von, 'Nachtrag zu der Abhand-lung über die im kaiserlichen Besitze befindlichen Cartone, darstellend Kaiser Karls V. Kriegszug nach Tunis, von Jan Vermayen', *Jahrbuch der kunsthistorischen Sammlungen des Allerhöchsten Kaiser-hauses*, vol. IX (Vienna, 1889), pp. 419–28 and vol. XI (Vienna, 1890), pp. 113–15.

Engerth, Eduard von, 'Über die im kunsthistori-schen Museum neu zur Aufstellung gelangenden Gemälde', *Jahrbuch der kunsthistorischen Sammlungen . . .*, vol. II (Vienna, 1884), pp. 145–66.

Fenaille, Maurice, *État général des tapisseries de la manufacture des Gobelins depuis son origine jusqu'à nos jours, 1600–1900*, vols. II and III, Paris, 1903, 1904.

Fortescue, Hon. Sir John William, *A History of the British Army*, London, Macmillan, 1899.

Fricx, H., *Carte des Pays Bas et des Frontières Françaises*, Brussels, 1712.

Geherig, Oscar, 'Das neue Badische Landesmuseum im Karlsruhe Residenzschloss', *Kunstchronik*, vol. XXXIII, pp. 93–9 (November 4th, 1921).

Göbel, Heinrich, *Wandteppiche*, Leipzig, 1923–1934.

Göbel, Heinrich, 'Die Geschichte Ottos von Wittels-bach: eine Wandteppichfolge', *Pantheon*, vol. V (April 1930), pp. 153–60.

Göbel, Heinrich, 'Wandteppichmanufakturen in Dänemark', *Cicerone*, vol. 18, Book 21 (November 1926), pp. 693–707.

Gómez Martínez, A., and Chillón Sampedro, B., *Los Tapices de la Catedral de Zamora*, Zamora, 1925.

Green, David, *Blenheim Palace*, London, Country Life Limited, 1951.

Guiffrey, Jean, and Marcel, P., *Inventaire général des dessins du Musée du Louvre et du Musée de Versailles*, Paris, 1907–[28] (vol. VIII).

Hofstede de Groot, Cornelis, *A Catalogue Raisonné of the works of the most eminent Dutch painters of the seventeenth century*, London, Macmillan, 1907–27 (vol. II).

Houdoy, Jules, *Tapisseries représentant la Conquête du Royaulme de Thunes par l'Empereur Charles-Quint*, Lille, 1873.

Huchtenberg, Jean, see Dumont.

Hunter, George Leland, *The Practical Book of Tapes-tries*, Philadelphia, 1925.

Jombert, Charles Antoine, *Catalogue raisonné de l'œuvre de S. Leclerc*, Paris, 1774 (pt. 2).

Jubinal, Michel Louis Achille, *Les anciennes tapisseries historiées etc.*, vol. I (Dijon), vol. II (Berne), Paris, 1838.

Keuller, H. F., and Wauters, Alphonse, *Les Tapis-series historiées à l'Exposition Nationale Belge de 1880*, Brussels, 1881.

Kotłubaj, Edward, *Galerie des portraits des Radziwill*, Vilna, 1857.

Kurth, Betty, 'Die Blütezeit der Bildwirkerkunst zu Tournai und der Burgundische Hof', *Jahrbuch der kunsthistorischen Sammlungen des Allerhöchsten Kaiser-hauses*, vol. XXXIV (Vienna and Leipzig, 1918), pp. 53–110.

Laborde, Léon Joseph Emmanuel Simon de, Mar-quis, *Les Ducs de Bourgogne*, Paris, 1849–52.

Liisberg, Bering, *The Royal Castle of Rosenborg; an illustrated guide*, Copenhagen, 1903.

'Lord Iveagh's Solebay Tapestries', *Country Life*, vol. LXV, pp. 351–3 (March 16th, 1929).

Loriquet, Charles, *Tapisseries de la Cathédrale de Reims*, Paris and Rheims, 1881.

Marillier, H. C., *English Tapestries of the Eighteenth Century*, London, Medici Society, 1930.

Marillier, H. C., 'The Tapestries of the Painted Chamber; the "Great History of Troy"', *Burlington Magazine*, vol. XLVI, pp. 35–42 (January 1925).

Mayer, Manfred, *Geschichte der Wandteppichfabriken des Wittelsbachischen Fürstenhauses in Bayern*, Munich, 1892.

Mérode Westerloo, Field-Marshal Count Jean Philippe Eugène, de, *Mémoires du Feld-Maréchal Comte de Mérode-Westerloo*, Brussels, 1840.

Morelowski, Marjan, *Gobelinz Wilénskie*, Vilna, 1933.

Müntz, Louis Frederic Eugène, *A Short History of Tapestry*, London, 1885.

Müntz, L. S. E., *Histoire générale de la Tapisserie*, Paris, 1878–85 (vol. II: Le Danemark, etc.).

Pinchart, Alexandre, *Histoire générale de la Tapisserie*, Paris, 1878–85 (vol. III: Pays-Bas).

Popham, A. E., 'Two fifteenth-century drawings for tapestry in the British Museum', *Burlington Magazine*, vol. XLV, pp. 60–6 (August 1924).

Renard, E., 'Die Bauten der Kurfürsten Joseph Clemens und Clemens August von Köln', *Bonner Jahrbücher*, No. XCIX, 1896, pp. 164–240.

Rott, Hans, 'Die Gobelins des Bruchsaler Schlosses', *Badische Heimat*, vol. IX, 1922.

Saxe, Eleanor B., 'Eighteenth Century Spanish Tapestries', *International Studio*, vol. 87 (August 1927), pp. 74–6.

Schmitz, Hermann, *Bildteppiche*, 3rd ed., Berlin, 1922.

Schumann, Paul, *Der Trojanische Krieg*, Dresden, 1898.

Seeley, *Stowe*, published in 1797.

Siegel, Vice-Admiral R., *Die Flagge*, Berlin, 1912.

Thieme-Becker, *Allgemeines Lexikon der bildenden Künstler*, Leipzig, 1907–47.

Thomson, William George, *Tapestry Weaving in England*, Batsford, London, 1915.

Trevelyan, George Macaulay, *England under Queen Anne*, vols. 1 and 2 (*Blenheim* and *Ramillies*), Collins Fontana Library, 1965.

Valencia de Don Juan, Count de, *Tapices de la Corona de España*, Madrid, 1903.

Wace, A. J. B., 'The unwoven tapestry of Ramillies', Oslo Kunstindustrimuseet *Årbok 1935, 1936, 1937*, pp. 53–66.

Wace, A. J. B., and Barnard, E. A. B., 'The Sheldon Tapestry Weavers and their Work', *Archaeologia*, vol. LXXVIII, 1928, pp. 255–314.

Wauters, Alphonse, *Bernard van Orley*, Paris, 1893.

Wauters, Alphonse, 'Essai Historique sur les Tapisseries de Bruxelles', *Bulletin des Commissions Royales d'Art et d'Archéologie*, Brussels, vol. XVI (1877).

Wauters, Alphonse, see Keuller.

Zimmermann, Eva, *Antike Textilien*, Karlsruhe, 1957.

Museum Publications

Berlin
Kunstgewerbe Museum, *Catalogue*, 1963.

Dublin
National Museum of Science and Art, *Museum Bulletin*, vol. IV, 1914, pt. 1.

Hamburg
Museum für Kunst und Gewerbe, *Bildteppiche aus 6 Jahrhunderten*, 1953.

Karlsruhe
Badisches Landesmuseum, *Meisterwerke*, 1959.

Lisbon
Boletim dos Museus Nacionais de Arte Antiga, vol. I, 1935, vol. II, 1942.

London
Victoria and Albert Museum, *Catalogue of Tapestries*, by A. F. Kendrick, 1914, 1924.

Schleissheim
Neues Schloss, *Amtlicher Führer*, Munich, 1965.

Stockholm
Nationalmuseets Utställningsblad, No. 3, 1918.

LIST OF ILLUSTRATIONS

LIST OF ILLUSTRATIONS

ILLUSTRATIONS IN APPENDIX III

INDEX OF ARTISTS

INDEX OF WEAVERS

INDEX OF FACTORIES

GENERAL INDEX

The page numbers in italics refer to names of tapestries.

INDEX